Quick & Easy
Thai

p

Contents

Introduction

Anyone who loves Thai food will appreciate that it is a unique cuisine, distinctly different from the cooking of the countries which border it, but with many culinary influences from far beyond its geographical frontiers. Thai cooking owes many of its characteristics to climate and culture, but a history of centuries of invasions and emigration has played a large part in shaping its cuisine. The roots of the Thai nation can be traced back to the first century, at the time of the Chinese Han Dynasty, when the T'ai tribes occupied parts of South China along valuable trade routes between the East and the West. Over the years, the T'ai had a close but often stormy relationship with the Chinese, and eventually began to emigrate south to the lands of what is now northern Thailand, bordering Burma and Cambodia, then sparsely occupied by Buddhist and Hindu communities.

In time, the T'ai established the independent Kingdom of Sukhothai (translated as "dawn of happiness"), which eventually became Siam. The ports of Siam were the entrance to an important trade route, and ships from all over Europe and Japan docked there, or sailed inland along the rivers, bringing foreign foods, teas, spices, silks, copper, and ceramics. In the 1500's, the Portuguese introduced the chile to South East Asia. The plant took immediately to the region's soils and climates, and continues to thrive. Trade with Arab and Indian merchants was important, and many Muslims settled in Siam.

The Kingdom of Siam survived until the 1939, when it became the constitutional Thai monarchy, and 21st-century Thailand still reflects much of her past centuries of mixed cultures. The Thai people are independent, proud, creative, and passionate. Their love of life is apparent in the way they take pleasure in entertaining and eating. They seem to a visitor to eat all day long. The streets and waterways are lined with food vendors selling a huge variety of tasty snacks from their stalls, carts, bicycles, and boats.

Thai people love parties and celebrations, and during their many festivals, the colorful, often elaborate and carefully prepared festive foods show a respect for custom and tradition. Visitors are entertained with an unending succession of trays of tasty snacks, platters of exotic fruits, and Thai beer, or local whiskey. When a meal is served, all the dishes are presented together, so the cook can enjoy the food along with the guests.

Thais take pride in presenting food beautifully. They carve vegetables and fruit into elaborate shapes as garnishes. Their intricate patterns and skilled artistry are an integral part of their culture, which exhibits a deep appreciation of beautiful things.

Everyday life in Thailand is closely tied to the seasons, marked by the harvesting of crops and the vagaries of the monsoon climate. The Thai people take food seriously, exercizing great care in choosing the freshest of ingredients, and thoughtfully balancing delicate flavors and textures. Throughout Thailand, rice is the most important staple food, the center of every meal. And coconut, in its various forms, has an almost equal place. Cooks in every region are expert at making the most of any ingredient available locally, so the character of many classic Thai dishes will vary according to the region in which they are cooked.

Fundamentals of Thai Cuisine

The essential ingredients you need to have in order to cook Thai food are listed below. Of these, the most important are coconut, lime, chile, rice, garlic, lemon grass, ginger root, and cilantro. With these you can create many traditional Thai dishes. Although many recipes have long lists of ingredients, the cooking methods involved in making them are simple enough even for inexperienced cooks to follow.

Balance is the guiding principle of Thai cooking, the five extremes of flavor, bitter, sour, hot, salt, and sweet, being carefully and skilfully balanced in every dish and over several courses. Each dish therefore contributes to the balance of the entire meal.

Basil Three varieties of sweet basil are used in Thai cooking, but the variety commonly sold in the West also works well. Asian food stores often sell the seeds for Thai basil, so you can grow your own.

Chiles The many varieties of chile vary from very mild to fiery hot, so choose carefully. The small red or green bird-eye chiles are often used in Thai dishes. They are very hot, and if you prefer a mild heat you should remove the seeds. Red chiles are generally slightly sweeter and milder than green. Larger chiles tend to be milder. Dried crushed chilis are used for seasoning.

Coconut Milk This is made from grated, pressed fresh coconut. It is sold very widely in cans and longlife packs, in powdered form, and in blocks as creamed coconut. Coconut cream is skimmed from the top, and is slightly thicker and richer.

Cilantro This is a fresh herb with a pungent, citrus-like flavor, widely used in savory dishes. It wilts quickly, so retains its freshness best if bought with a root attached. Alternatively, you can grow your own.

Galangal A relative of ginger, with a milder, aromatic flavor. Galangal is available fresh or dried.

Garlic The pungent cloves of this bulb are used abundantly in Thai cooking, whole, crushed, sliced, or chopped, in savory dishes, and in curry pastes. Fresh garlic can be bought widely, but pickled garlic is a useful purchase because it makes an attractive garnish.

Ginger

Fresh ginger root is peeled, grated, chopped or sliced for a warm spicy flavor.

Kaffir Lime Leaves

These leaves have a distinctive lime scent, and can be bought fresh, dried, and frozen.

Lemon Grass

An aromatic tropical grass with a lemon scent similar to lemon balm. Strip off the fibrous outer leaves and slice or chop the insides finely, or bruise and use whole. Lemon grass can also be bought dried in powdered form.

Palm Sugar

This is a rich, brown, unrefined sugar made from the coconut palm and sold in solid blocks. The best way to use it is to crush it with a mallet or a rolling pin. Fstl ntpem sugar is a good substitute.

Rice Vinegar

Mirin, or sweet rice vinegar, is a savory flavoring. Sherry or white wine vinegar can be substituted.

Soy Sauce

Dark and light soy sauce are used for seasoning. The light sauce is saltier than the dark and is used mainly in stir-fries and with light meats. Dark soy sauce adds a mature rich flavor and color to braised and red meat dishes.

Tamarind Paste

The pulp of the tamarind fruit is usually sold in blocks. It gives a sour/sweet flavor. Soak the pulp in hot water for 30 minutes, press out the juice, and discard pulp and seeds.

Thai Fish Sauce

Called *nam pla*, this is used like salt for seasoning, and has a distinctive, intense aroma. It is made from salted fermented fish.

KEY	
	Simplicity level 1–3 (1 easiest, 3 slightly harder)
	Preparation time
	Cooking time

Thai-Style Seafood Soup

Because taste and tolerance for chilis varies, use chili paste. It enables you to control the degree of heat in this dish.

NUTRITIONAL INFORMATION

Calories 132   Sugars 7g
Protein ....20g   Fat 2g
Carbohydrate ....9g   Saturates 0.1g

🍲 10–15 mins   🕐 25 mins

SERVES 4

I N G R E D I E N T S

5 cups fish bouillon

1 lemon grass stem, split lengthwise

pared rind of ½ lime, or 1 lime leaf

1 inch/2.5 cm piece fresh root ginger, peeled and sliced

¼ tsp chilli paste, or to taste

4–6 scallions, sliced

7 oz/200 g large of mediumshrimp, peeled

9 oz/250 g scallops (16–20)

2 tbsp fresh cilantro

salt

finely chopped red bell pepper, or red chile rings, to garnish

1 Put the bouillon in a saucepan with the lemon grass, lime rind or leaf, ginger, and chili paste. Bring just to a boil, reduce the heat, cover, and simmer for 10–15 minutes.

COOK'S TIP

If you have light chicken bouillon, but no fish bouillon, the chicken bouillon will make an equally tasty though different version of this soup.

2 Cut the baby leek in half lengthwise, then slice crosswise very thinly. Cut the shrimp almost in half lengthwise, keeping the tail intact.

3 Strain the bouillon, return to the saucepan and bring to a simmer, with bubbles rising at the edges and the surface trembling. Add the leek and cook for 2–3 minutes. Season with salt, if needed, and stir in chili paste if wished.

4 Add the scallops and shrimp and poach for about 1 minute until they turn opaque and the shrimp curl.

5 Drop in the fresh cilantro leaves, ladle the soup into warm bowls, dividing the shellfish evenly, and garnish the soup with red bell pepper or red chile rings.

Chicken & Coconut Soup

Make this soup when you want a change from traditional chicken soup. It is nicely spiced and garnished with a generous quantity of cilantro leaves.

NUTRITIONAL INFORMATION

Calories 76	Sugars 2g	
Protein 13g	Fat 1g	
Carbohydrate 3g	Saturates 0.1g	

15 mins   30–45 mins

SERVES 4

INGREDIENTS

5 cups chicken bouillon

7 oz/200 g skinless boned chicken

1 chile, split lengthwise
  and deseeded

3 inch/7.5 cm piece lemon grass,
  split lengthwise

3–4 lime leaves

1 inch/2.5 cm piece fresh root ginger,
  peeled and sliced

½ cup coconut milk

6–8 scallions, sliced diagonally

¼ tsp chilli paste, or to taste

salt

fresh cilantro leaves, to garnish

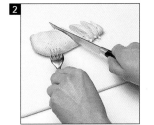

1 Put the bouillon in a pan with the chicken, chile, lemon grass, lime leaves and ginger. Bring almost to a boil, reduce the heat, cover, and simmer for 20–25 minutes, or until the chicken is cooked through and firm to the touch.

2 Remove the chicken and strain the bouillon. When the chicken is cool, slice thinly or shred into bite-size pieces.

3 Return the bouillon to the saucepan and heat to simmering. Stir in the coconut milk and scallions. Add the

chicken and continue simmering for about 10 minutes, until the soup is heated through and the flavors have mingled.

4 Stir in the chili paste. Season to taste with salt and, if wished, add a little more chili paste.

5 Ladle the soup into warm bowls and float a few fresh cilantro leaves on top of the soup tp serve.

COOK'S TIP
Once the bouillon is flavored and the chicken cooked, this soup is very quick to finish. If you wish, poach the chicken and strain the bouillon ahead of time. Store in the refrigerator separately.

Cold Cilantro Soup

This soup brings together Thai flavors for a cool refreshing starter. It highlights fresh cilantro, now very widely available.

NUTRITIONAL INFORMATION

Calories 79   Sugars 5g
Protein ....3g   Fat 3g
Carbohydrate ...13g   Saturates 0.1g

 10 mins   35–40 mins

SERVES 4

INGREDIENTS

2 tsp olive oil

1 large onion, finely chopped

1 leek, thinly sliced

1 garlic clove, thinly sliced

4 cups water

1 zucchini, about 7 oz/200 g, peeled and chopped

4 tbsp white rice

2 inch/5 cm piece lemon grass

2 lime leaves

1 cup fresh cilantro leaves and soft stems

chili paste, (optional)

salt and pepper

finely chopped red bell pepper and/or red chiles, to garnish

1 Heat the oil in a large saucepan over a medium heat. Add the onion, leek, and garlic, cover, and cook for 4–5 minutes until the onion is softened, stirring frequently.

2 Add the water, zucchini, and rice with a large pinch of salt and some pepper. Stir in the lemon grass and lime leaves. Bring just to a boil and reduce the heat to low. Cover and simmer for about 15–20 minutes until the rice is soft and tender.

3 Add the cilantro leaves, pushing them down into the liquid. Continue cooking for 2–3 minutes until they are wilted. Remove the lemon grass and lime leaves.

4 Let the soup cool slightly, then transfer to a blender or food processor and purée until smooth.

5 Scrape the soup into a large container. Season to taste with salt and pepper. Cover and refrigerate until cold.

6 Taste and adjust the seasoning. For a more spicy soup, stir in a little chili to taste. For a thinner soup, add a small amount of iced water. Ladle into chilled bowls and garnish with finely chopped red bell pepper and/or chiles.

Thai Fish Soup

This is also known as Tom Yam Gung. Asian supermarkets may sell tom yam sauce ready prepared in jars, sometimes labeled "Chilis in Oil."

NUTRITIONAL INFORMATION

Calories . . . . . . .230 Sugars 4g
Protein . . . . .22g Fat 12g
Carbohydrate . . . .9g Saturates 1g

25 mins   20 mins

SERVES 4

INGREDIENTS

2 cups light chicken bouillon

2 lime leaves, chopped

2 inch/5 cm piece lemon grass, chopped

3 tbsp lemon juice

3 tbsp Thai fish sauce

2 small, hot green chiles, deseeded and finely chopped

½ tsp sugar

8 small shiitake mushrooms or 8 straw mushrooms, halved

1 lb/450 g raw shrimp, peeled if necessary and de-veined

scallions, to garnish

TOM YAM SAUCE

4 tbsp vegetable oil

5 garlic cloves, finely chopped

1 large shallot, finely chopped

2 large hot dried red chiles, coarsely chopped

1 tbsp dried shrimp (optional)

1 tbsp Thai fish sauce

2 tsp sugar

1 First make the tom yam sauce. Heat the oil in a small skillet and add the garlic. Cook for a few seconds until the garlic just browns. Remove with a slotted spoon and set aside. Add the shallot to the same oil and cook until browned and crisp. Remove with a slotted spoon and set aside. Add the chiles and cook until they darken. Remove from the oil and drain on paper towels. Remove the skillet from the burner, reserve the oil.

2 In a small food processor or spice grinder, grind the dried shrimp, if using, then add the reserved chiles, garlic, and shallots. Grind together to a smooth paste. Return the skillet with the original oil to a low heat, add the paste, and warm. Add the fish sauce and sugar and mix. Remove from the heat.

3 In a large saucepan, heat together the bouillon and 2 tablespoons of the tom yam sauce. Add the lime leaves, lemon grass, lemon juice, fish sauce, chiles, and sugar. Simmer for 2 minutes.

4 Add the mushrooms and shrimp and cook an additional 2–3 minutes until the shrimp are cooked. Ladle into warm soup bowls and serve immediately garnished with scallions.

Corn & Crab Soup with Egg

This speedy soup is a good standby, made in a matter of minutes.
If you prefer, you can use frozen crab sticks.

NUTRITIONAL INFORMATION

Calories 183   Sugars 9g
Protein ....7g   Fat 6g
Carbohydrate ...26g   Saturates 1g

xx mins   xx mins

SERVES 4

INGREDIENTS

1 tbsp vegetable oil

3 garlic cloves, crushed

1 tsp fresh ginger root, grated

3 cups chicken bouillon

13 oz/375 g canned creamed corn

1 tbsp Thai fish sauce

6 oz/175 g canned white crabmeat, drained

1 egg

salt and pepper

fresh cilantro, shredded, and paprika, to garnish

1 Heat the vegetable oil in a large saucepan and cook the garlic for 1 minute, stirring constantly.

2 Add the ginger, then stir in the bouillon and corn. Bring to a boil.

3 Stir in the fish sauce, crabmeat, and season with the salt and pepper, then return the soup to a boil.

4 Beat the egg, then stir lightly into the soup so that it sets into long strands. Simmer gently for about 30 seconds until just set.

5 Ladle the soup into bowls and serve hot, garnished with shredded fresh cilantro leaves and paprika sprinkled over.

COOK'S TIP

To give the soup an extra rich flavor kick for a special occasion, stir in 1 tablespoon of dry sherry or rice wine just before you ladle it into warm soup bowls.

Pumpkin & Coconut Soup

This substantial soup is filling and, if served with crusty bread, is all you need for a satisfying lunch.

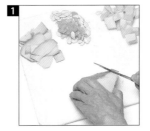

NUTRITIONAL INFORMATION

Calories 105	Sugars 6g
Protein 3g	Fat 7g
Carbohydrate 8g	Saturates 4g

  20 mins 45–50 mins

SERVES 6

I N G R E D I E N T S

2 lb 4 oz/1 kg pumpkin

1 tbsp peanut oil

1 tsp yellow mustard seeds

1 garlic clove, crushed

1 large onion, chopped

1 celery stalk, chopped

1 small red chile, chopped

3¾ cups bouillon

1 tbsp dried prawns

5 tbsp coconut cream

salt and pepper

extra coconut cream, to garnish

1 Halve the pumpkin and remove the seeds. Cut away the skin and dice the pumpkin flesh.

2 Heat the oil in a large flameproof casserole and cook the mustard seeds until they begin to pop. Stir in the garlic, onion, celery, and chile, and stir-fry them for 1–2 minutes.

3 Add the pumpkin with the bouillon and dried shrimp and bring to a boil. Lower the heat, cover, and simmer gently for about 30 minutes until the ingredients are very tender.

4 Transfer the mixture to a food processor or blender, and process until smooth. Return the mixture to the pan and stir in the coconut cream.

5 Adjust the seasoning to taste with salt and pepper and serve hot, with coconut cream swirled in each bowl. For an extra touch of garnish, swirl a spoonful of thick coconut milk into each bowl of soup as you serve it.

Mushroom & Tofu Broth

Dried black mushrooms are sold in Asian stores, and although they can be expensive, they are worth searching out.

NUTRITIONAL INFORMATION

Calories	65	Sugars	.........1g
Protein	.........4g	Fat	...........5g
Carbohydrate	....2g	Saturates	.......1g

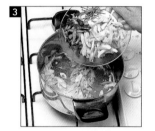

 10 mins   1–15 mins

SERVES 4

INGREDIENTS

4 dried black mushrooms

1 tbsp sunflower oil

1 tsp sesame oil

1 garlic clove, crushed

1 green chile, deseeded and finely chopped

6 scallions

4 cups rich brown bouillon

1½ cups fresh oyster mushrooms, sliced

2 kaffir lime leaves, finely shredded

2 tbsp lime juice

1 tbsp rice vinegar

1 tbsp Thai fish sauce

½ cup firm tofu, diced

salt and pepper

COOK'S TIP

Stock cubes make a cloudy broth, so use a clear, richly colored homemade beef bouillon, or a Japanese dashi. For a vegetarian broth, use a well-flavored vegetable bouillon and light soy sauce.

1 Pour ⅔ cup boiling water over the dried black mushrooms in a heatproof bowl and let soak for about 30 minutes. Drain, reserving the liquid, then chop the black mushrooms coarsely.

2 Heat the sunflower and sesame oils in a large pan or wok over a high heat. Add the garlic, chile, and scallions, and stir for 1 minute until they are softened but not browned.

3 Add the mushrooms, lime leaves, bouillon, and reserved mushroom liquid. Bring to a boil.

4 Stir in the lime juice, rice vinegar, and fish sauce, lower the heat and simmer gently for 3–4 minutes.

5 Add the diced tofu and adjust the seasoning to taste. Heat gently until boiling, then serve immediately.

Rice Soup with Eggs

This version of a classic Thai soup, sometimes eaten for breakfast, is a good way of using up any leftover cooked rice.

NUTRITIONAL INFORMATION

Calories 197   Sugars 1g
Protein ....11g   Fat 10g
Carbohydrate ...17g   Saturates 2g

     10 mins   20 mins

SERVES 4

I N G R E D I E N T S

1 tsp sunflower oil

1 garlic clove, crushed

1¾ oz/50 g ground pork

3 scallions, sliced

1 tbsp fresh ginger root, grated

1 red bird-eye chile, deseeded and chopped

4 cups chicken bouillon

1¼ cups cooked long-grain rice

1 tbsp Thai fish sauce

4 small eggs

salt and pepper

2 tbsp fresh cilantro, shredded, to garnish

1 Heat the oil in a large skillet or wok. Add the garlic and pork and cook gently for about 1 minute until the meat is broken up but not browned.

2 Stir in the scallions, ginger, chile, and chicken bouillon, stirring until boiling. Add the rice, lower the heat,, and simmer for 2 minutes.

3 Add the fish sauce and adjust the seasoning with salt and pepper to taste. Carefully break the eggs into the soup and simmer over a very low heat for 3–4 minutes until set.

4 Ladle the soup into large bowls, allowing 1 egg per portion. Garnish with shredded cilantro and serve immediately.

COOK'S TIP
If you prefer, beat the eggs together and cook them like an omelet until set, then cut into ribbonlike strips and add to the soup just before serving.

Spinach & Ginger Soup

This mildly spiced, rich green soup is delicately scented with ginger and lemon grass. It makes a good light appetizer or summer lunch dish.

NUTRITIONAL INFORMATION

Calories	38	Sugars	. . . . .0.8g
Protein	. . . . .3.2g	Fat	. . . . .1.8g
Carbohydrate	. . .2.4g	Saturates	. . . . .0.2g

 xx mins   xx mins

SERVES 4

INGREDIENTS

2 tbsp sunflower oil

1 onion, chopped

2 garlic cloves, finely chopped

1 inch/2.5 cm piece ginger root,
    finely chopped

4 cups fresh young spinach leaves

1 small lemon grass stem,
    finely chopped

4 cups chicken or vegetable bouillon

1 small potato, peeled and chopped

1 tbsp rice wine or dry sherry

1 tsp sesame oil

salt and pepper

fresh spinach, finely shredded, to garnish

1 Heat the oil in a large pan. Add the onion, garlic, and ginger, and cook gently for 3–4 minutes until softened.

2 Reserve 2–3 small spinach leaves. Add the remaining leaves and lemon grass to the pan, stirring until the spinach is wilted. Add the bouillon and potato to the pan and bring to a boil. Lower the heat, cover, and simmer for about 10 minutes.

3 Tip the soup into a blender or a food processor and blend until smooth.

4 Return to the pan, and add the rice wine. Season to taste. Heat until just about to boil.

5 Shred the reserved spinach leaves finely and scatter over the soup. Drizzle with a little sesame oil and serve.

VARIATION

To make a creamy spinach and coconut soup, stir in 4 tablespoons creamed coconut, or replace about 1¼ cups of bouillon with coconut milk. Scatter fresh coonut shavings over it.

Chilled Avocado Soup

A delightfully simple soup with a blend of typical Thai flavors, which needs no cooking and can be served at any time of day.

NUTRITIONAL INFORMATION

Calories ....188 Sugars 2g
Protein ....3g Fat 18g
Carbohydrate ....4g Saturates 5g

  1–15 mins   0 mins

SERVES 4

INGREDIENTS

2 ripe avocados

1 small mild onion, chopped

1 garlic clove, crushed

2 tbsp fresh cilantro, chopped

1 tbsp fresh mint, chopped

2 tbsp lime juice

3 cups vegetable bouillon

1 tbsp rice vinegar

1 tbsp light soy sauce

salt and pepper

GARNISH

2 tbsp sour cream or crème fraîche

1 tbsp fresh cilantro, finely chopped

2 tsp lime juice

lime rind, finely shredded

1 Halve, pit, and scoop out the flesh from the avocados. Place in a blender or food processor with the onion, garlic, cilantro, mint, lime juice, and about half the bouillon, and process until completely smooth.

2 Add the remaining bouillon, rice vinegar, and soy sauce and blend again to mix well. Taste and adjust seasoning if necessary with salt and pepper, or with a little extra lime juice if required. Cover and chill in the refrigerator until needed.

3 To make the lime and cilantro cream garnish, mix together the sour cream, cilantro and lime juice. Spoon into the soup just before serving and sprinkle with lime rind.

COOK'S TIP

The surface of the soup may darken if it is stored for longer than an hour. Stir ot before serving. If you plan to keep the soup for several hours, lay plastic wrap over the surface to seal it.

Shrimp Satay

There are no substitutes for lemon grass and lime leaves, which give these shrimp kabobs their authentic Thai flavor.

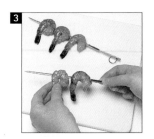

NUTRITIONAL INFORMATION

Calories	367	Sugars	........25g
Protein	.........9g	Fat	..........23g
Carbohydrate	...33g	Saturates	.......3g

  15 mins   15–20 mins

SERVES 4

I N G R E D I E N T S

12 peeled raw jumbo shrimp

M A R I N A D E

1 tsp ground coriander

1 tsp ground cumin

2 tbsp light soy sauce

4 tbsp vegetable oil

1 tbsp curry powder

1 tbsp ground turmeric

½ cup coconut milk

3 tbsp sugar

P E A N U T   S A U C E

2 tbsp vegetable oil

3 garlic cloves, crushed

1 tbsp red curry paste (see Red Shrimp Curry, page 102)

½ cup coconut milk

1 cup fish or chicken bouillon

1 tbsp sugar

1 tsp salt

1 tbsp lemon juice

4 tbsp unsalted roasted peanuts, finely chopped

4 tbsp dried breadcrumbs

1 Slit the shrimp down their backs and remove the black vein, if any. Set aside. Mix the marinade ingredients and add the prawns. Mix well, cover, and set aside for at least 8 hours or overnight.

2 To make the peanut sauce, heat the oil in a large skillet until very hot. Add the garlic and cook until it starts to color. Add the curry paste and mix well. Cook for 30 seconds. Add the coconut milk, sugar, salt,, and lemon juice, and stir well. Boil for 1–2 minutes, stirring constantly. Add the peanuts and bread crumbs, and mix well. Pour the sauce into a bowl and set aside.

3 Using 4 skewers, thread 3 prawns onto each. Cook under a preheated hot broiler or on the barbecue for about 3–4 minutes on each side until just cooked through. Serve immediately with the peanut sauce.

Sweet & Sour Fish Cakes

If you can find them, use small chiles, called bird-eye, for the dipping sauce. They are very hot however, so remove the seeds if you prefer.

NUTRITIONAL INFORMATION

Calories 213   Sugars 23g
Protein . . . . .21g   Fat 4g
Carbohydrate . . .25g   Saturates 1g

 15 mins   ⊘ 10 mins

SERVES 4

INGREDIENTS

1 lb/450 g firm white fish, such as hake, haddock, or cod, skinned and coarsely chopped

1 tbsp Thai fish sauce

1 tbsp red curry paste (see Red Shrimp Curry, page 47)

1 kaffir lime leaf, finely shredded

2 tbsp chopped fresh cilantro

1 egg

1 tsp brown sugar

large pinch salt

½ cup green beans, thinly sliced crosswise

vegetable oil, for shallow-frying

SWEET-AND-SOUR DIPPING SAUCE

4 tbsp sugar

1 tbsp cold water

3 tbsp white rice vinegar

2 small, hot chiles, finely chopped

1 tbsp fish sauce

1 For the fish cakes, put the fish, fish sauce, curry paste, lime leaf, cilantro, egg, sugar, and salt into a food processor. Process until smooth. Scrape into a bowl and stir in the green beans. Set aside.

2 To make the dipping sauce, put the sugar, water, and rice vinegar into a pan and heat gently until the sugar has dissolved. Bring to a boil and simmer for 2 minutes. Remove from the heat and stir in the chiles and fish sauce and let to cool.

3 Heat a skillet with enough oil to cover the bottom. Divide the fish mixture into 16 balls. Flatten the balls into patties and cook in hot oil for 1–2 minutes each side until golden. Drain on paper towels. Serve hot with the dipping sauce.

COOK'S TIP
It isn't necessary to use the most expensive cut of white fish in this recipe since the other flavors are very strong. Use whatever is cheapest.

Thai Noodles

This is a delicious classic Thai noodle dish, flavored with fish sauce, roasted peanuts, and shrimp.

NUTRITIONAL INFORMATION

Calories	344	Sugars	.........2g
Protein	........21g	Fat	..........17g
Carbohydrate	...27g	Saturates	.......2g

 20 mins   10–15 mins

SERVES 4

INGREDIENTS

12 oz/350 g cooked, peeled jumbo shrimp

4 oz/115 g flat rice noodles or
 rice vermicelli

4 tbsp vegetable oil

2 garlic cloves, finely chopped

1 egg

2 tbsp lemon juice

1½ tbsp Thai fish sauce

½ tsp sugar

2 tbsp chopped, roasted peanuts

½ tsp cayenne pepper

2 scallions, cut into
 1 inch/2.5 cm pieces

½ cup fresh beansprouts

1 tbsp chopped cilantro

lemon wedges, to serve

1 Drain the shrimp on paper towels to remove excess moisture. Cook the noodles. Drain well and set aside.

2 Heat the oil in a skillet. Cook the garlic until golden. Add the egg and stir to break it up. Cook for a few seconds.

3 Add the shrimp and noodles, mixing them well with the egg and garlic.

4 Add the lemon juice, fish sauce, sugar, half the peanuts, cayenne pepper, scallions, and half the beansprouts, stirring quickly all the time. Cook over a high heat for an additional 2 minutes.

5 Turn the mixture onto a serving plate. Top with the remaining peanuts and the beansprouts and sprinkle with the cilantro. Serve with lemon wedges.

VARIATION

This is a basic dish to which lots of different cooked seafood could be added. Cooked squid rings, mussels, and langoustines would all work just as well as the shrimp.

Fish Cakes with Hot Sauce

These little fish cakes are very popular in Thailand as street food, and make a perfect snack. Also serve them as an appetizer.

NUTRITIONAL INFORMATION

Calories	205	Sugars	.........6g
Protein	........17g	Fat	..........12g
Carbohydrate	....7g	Saturates	.......2g

 10 mins   15–20 mins

SERVES 4–5

INGREDIENTS

12 oz/350 g white fish fillet without skin, such as cod or haddock

1 tbsp Thai fish sauce

2 tsp Thai red curry paste

1 tbsp lime juice

1 garlic clove, crushed

4 dried kaffir lime leaves, crumbled

1 egg white

3 tbsp fresh cilantro, chopped

salt and pepper

vegetable oil for shallow frying

green salad leaves, to serve

PEANUT DIP

1 small red chile

1 tbsp light soy sauce

1 tbsp lime juice

1 tbsp brown sugar

3 tbsp crunchy peanut butter

4 tbsp coconut milk

1 Put the fish fillet in a food processor with the fish sauce, curry paste, lime juice, garlic, lime leaves, and egg white, and process until a smooth paste forms.

2 Stir in the cilantro and process until mixed. Divide the mixture into 8–10 pieces and roll into balls. Flatten to make round patties and set aside.

3 For the dip, deseed and finely chop the chile. Place in a pan with the remaining ingredients and heat gently, stirring constantly. Adjust the seasoning.

4 Shallow cook the fish cakes for 3–4 minutes on each side until golden brown. Drain on paper towels and serve hot on a bed of green salad with the dip.

Thai-Style Crab Sandwich

A hearty, open sandwich, topped with a classic flavor combination crab with avocado and ginger. Perfect for a light summer lunch.

NUTRITIONAL INFORMATION

Calories . . . . . . .768 Sugars 3g
Protein . . . . .26g Fat 49g
Carbohydrate . . .58g Saturates 8g

 xx mins   xx mins

SERVES 2

INGREDIENTS

2 tbsp lime juice

¾ inch/2 cm piece fresh ginger root, grated

¾ inch/2 cm piece lemon grass, finely chopped

5 tbsp mayonnaise

2 large slices crusty bread

1 ripe avocado

1 cup cooked crabmeat

black pepper, freshly ground

sprigs fresh cilantro, to garnish

1 Mix half the lime juice with the ginger and lemon grass. Add the mayonnaise and mix well.

2 Spread 1 tablespoon of mayonnaise smoothly over each slice of bread.

3 Halve the avocado and remove the pit. Peel and slice the flesh thinly,, then arrange the avocado slices on the slices of bread. Sprinkle the lime juice. liberally over the avocado.

4 Spoon the cooked crabmeat over the avocado, then add any remaining lime juice. Spoon the remaining mayonnaise over the sandwiches, and season them with freshly ground black pepper,. Top with a fresh sprig of cilantro, and serve the sandwiches immediately.

COOK'S TIP

To make lime-and-ginger mayonnaise, place 2 egg yolks, 1 tablespoon lime juice, and ½ teaspoon grated ginger root in a blender. With the motor running, add 1¼ cups olive oil, drop by drop, until thick and smooth, and season.

Sticky Ginger Chicken Wings

A finger-licking appetizer for chicken wings or drumsticks. It is perfect for parties (have finger bowls ready).

NUTRITIONAL INFORMATION

Calories . . . . .416 Sugars 5g
Protein . . . . .41g Fat 25g
Carbohydrate . . . .7g Saturates 7g

30 mins   12–15 mins

SERVES 4

INGREDIENTS

2 garlic cloves, peeled

1 piece candied ginger in syrup

1 tsp coriander seeds

2 tbsp candied ginger syrup

2 tbsp dark soy sauce

1 tbsp lime juice

1 tsp sesame oil

12 chicken wings

lime wedges and fresh cilantro leaves, to garnish

1 Chop the garlic and candied ginger coarsely. In a pestle and mortar, crush the garlic, candied ginger, and coriander seeds to a paste, gradually working in the ginger syrup, soy sauce, lime juice, and sesame oil.

2 Tuck the pointed tip of each chicken wing underneath the thicker end of the wing to make a neat triangular shape. Place in a large bowl.

3 Add the garlic and ginger paste to the bowl and toss the chicken wings in the mixture to coat evenly. Cover and put in the refrigerator to marinate for several hours or overnight.

4 Arrange the chicken wings in one layer on a tinfoil-lined broiler pan and broil under a medium-hot grill for 12–15 minutes, turning them occasionally, until golden brown and cooked through.

5 Alternatively, cook on a lightly oiled barbecue grill over medium-hot coals for 12–15 minutes. To serve, garnish with lime wedges and fresh cilantro.

COOK'S TIP
To test if the chicken is cooked, pierce it deeply through the thickest part of the flesh. If it is cooked, the chicken juices are clear, with no trace of pink.

Lemon Grass Chicken

An unusual recipe in which fresh lemon grass stems are used as skewers, which impart their delicate lemon flavor to the chicken.

NUTRITIONAL INFORMATION

Calories 140	Sugars 2g	
Protein 19g	Fat 7g	
Carbohydrate 2g	Saturates 1g	

25 mins   4–6 mins

SERVES 4

INGREDIENTS

2 long or 4 short lemon grass stems

2 large boneless, skinless chicken breasts, about 14 oz/400 g in total

1 small egg white

1 carrot, finely grated

1 small red chile, deseeded and chopped

2 tbsp fresh garlic chives, chopped

2 tbsp fresh cilantro, chopped

1 tbsp sunflower oil

salt and pepper

cilantro and lime slices, to garnish

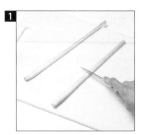

1 If the lemon grass stems are long, cut them in half across the middle to make 4 short lengths. Cut each stalk in half lengthwise, so that you have 8 sticks.

COOK'S TIP

If you can't find whole lemon grass stalks (stems), use wooden or bamboo skewers instead, and add ½ teaspoon ground lemon grass to the mixture with the other flavourings.

2 Chop the chicken coarsely and place in a food processor with the egg white. Process to a smooth paste. Add the carrot, chile, chives, cilantro, and salt and pepper. Process for a few seconds to mix.

3 Chill the mixture in the refrigerator for about 15 minutes. Divide the mixture into 8 equal portions, and use your hands to shape the mixture around the lemon grass "skewers."

4 Brush the skewers with oil and broil under a preheated medium-hot broiler for 4–6 minutes, turning them occasionally, until golden brown and thoroughly cooked. Alternatively, barbecue over medium-hot coals.

5 Serve hot, and garnish with cilantro and slices of lime.

Thai Stuffed Omelet

This makes a substantial appetizer, or a light lunch or supper dish. Serve with a colorful, crisp salad to accompany the dish.

NUTRITIONAL INFORMATION

Calories 270	Sugars 1g
Protein 24g	Fat 18g
Carbohydrate 2g	Saturates 4g

10 mins   30–40 mins

SERVES 4

INGREDIENTS

2 garlic cloves, chopped

4 black peppercorns

4 sprigs fresh cilantro

2 tbsp vegetable oil

7 oz/200 g ground pork

2 scallions, chopped

1 large, firm tomato, chopped

6 large eggs

1 tbsp Thai fish sauce

¼ tsp turmeric

mixed salad leaves, tossed, to serve

1 Place the garlic, peppercorns, and cilantro in a pestle and mortar and crush until a smooth paste forms

2 Heat 1 tablespoon of oil in a wok over a medium heat. Add the paste and fry for 1–2 minutes until it just changes color.

3 Stir in the pork and stir-fry until it is lightly browned. Add the scallions and tomato, and stir-fry for another minute, then remove from the heat.

4 Heat the remaining oil in a skillet. Beat the eggs with the fish sauce and turmeric, then pour a quarter of the egg mixture into the skillet. As the mixture begins to set, stir it very lightly to ensure that all the liquid egg is set.

5 Spoon a quarter of the pork mixture down the center of the omelette, then fold the sides in toward the center, enclosing the filling. Make 3 more omelets.

6 Slide the omelets onto a serving plate and serve with a mixed salad.

COOK'S TIP

If you prefer, spread half the pork mixture evenly over one omelet, then place a second omelet on top, without folding. Cut into slim wedges to serve.

Thai-Spiced Sausages

These mildly spiced little sausages are ideal for a buffet meal. They can be made a day in advance and are equally good served hot or cold.

NUTRITIONAL INFORMATION

Calories	206	Sugars	.......0.1g
Protein	........22g	Fat	...........11g
Carbohydrate	....4g	Saturates	.......2g

 2–25 mins   8–10 mins

SERVES 4

I N G R E D I E N T S

14 oz/400 g lean ground pork

4 tbsp cooked rice

1 garlic clove, crushed

1 tsp Thai red curry paste

1 tsp ground black pepper

1 tsp ground coriander

½ tsp salt

3 tbsp lime juice

2 tbsp fresh cilantro, chopped

3 tbsp peanut oil

coconut sambal or soy sauce, to serve

1 Place the pork, rice, garlic, curry paste, pepper, coriander, salt, lime juice, and cilantro in a bowl and knead together with your hands to mix evenly.

2 Shape the mixture into 12 small link shapes. If you can buy sausage casings, fill the casings and twist at intervals to separate the sausages.

3 Heat the oil in a large skillet over a medium heat. Add the sausages, in batches if necessary, and fry for 8–10 minutes, turning them over occasionally, until they are evenly golden brown. Serve hot with a coconut sambal or soy sauce.

COOK'S TIP

These sausages can also be served as an appetizer—shape the mixture slightly smaller to make about 16 bite-size sausages. Serve with a soy dip.

Thai-Style Burgers

If your family likes to eat burgers, try these—they have a much more interesting flavor than conventional hamburgers.

NUTRITIONAL INFORMATION

Calories	358	Sugars	.........1g
Protein	........23g	Fat	..........29g
Carbohydrate	....2g	Saturates	.......5g

20 mins   6–8 mins

SERVES 4

INGREDIENTS

1 small lemon grass stem

1 small red chile, deseeded

2 garlic cloves, peeled

2 scallions

2½ cups closed-cup mushrooms

14 oz/400 g ground pork

1 tbsp Thai fish sauce

3 tbsp fresh cilantro, chopped

sunflower oil for shallow frying

2 tbsp mayonnaise

1 tbsp lime juice

salt and pepper

TO SERVE

4 sesame hamburger buns

shredded Napa cabbage

1 Place the lemon grass, chile, garlic and scallions in a food processor and process to a smooth paste. Add the mushrooms, and process until they are very finely chopped.

2 Add the ground pork, fish sauce, and cilantro. Season well with salt and pepper, then divide the mixture into 4 equal portions and shape with lightly floured hands into flat burger shapes.

3 Heat the oil in a skillet over a medium heat. Add the burgers and fry for 6–8 minutes until done or as you like.

4 Meanwhile, mix the mayonnaise with the lime juice. Split the hamburger buns and spread the lime-flavored mayonnaise on the cut surfaces. Add some shredded Napa cabbage, top with a burger, and sandwich together. Serve immediately, while still hot.

COOK'S TIP

You can add a spoonful of your favorite relish to each burger, or alternatively, add a few pieces of crisp pickled vegetables for a change of texture.

Hot & Sour Noodles

This simple, fast-food dish is sold from street food stalls in Thailand, with many and varied additions of meat and vegetables.

NUTRITIONAL INFORMATION

Calories	337	Sugars	.........1g
Protein	........10g	Fat	...........11g
Carbohydrate	...53g	Saturates	.......1g

 10 mins   10–15 mins

SERVES 4

INGREDIENTS

9 oz/250 g dried medium egg noodles

1 tbsp sesame oil

1 tbsp chili oil

1 garlic clove, crushed

2 scallions, finely chopped

⅔ cup button mushrooms, sliced

1 cup dried Chinese black mushrooms, soaked, drained, and sliced

2 tbsp lime juice

3 tbsp light soy sauce

1 tsp sugar

TO SERVE

shredded Napa cabbage

2 tbsp shredded cilantro

2 tbsp toasted peanuts, chopped

COOK'S TIP

Thai chili oil is very hot, so if you want a milder flavor, use vegetable oil for the initial cooking instead, then add a final dribble of chili oil just for seasoning.

1 Cook the noodles in a large pan of boiling water for about 3–4 minutes, or according to the directions on the package. Drain well and return to the pan,, then toss the noodles with the sesame oil and set them aside.

2 Heat the chili oil in a large skillet or wok and quickly stir-fry the garlic, scallions, and button mushrooms until they are softened but not browned.

3 Add the black mushrooms, lime juice, soy sauce, and sugar. and continue stir-frying until the mixture boils. Add the noodles and toss to mix.

4 Serve the hot-and-sour noodles spooned over Napa cabbage, sprinkled with cilantro and peanuts.

Pad Thai Noodles

The combination of ingredients in this classic dish varies, depending on the cook, but it commonly contains a mixture of pork and shrimp.

NUTRITIONAL INFORMATION

Calories 477	Sugars 6g
Protein 26g	Fat 14g
Carbohydrate ...60g	Saturates 3g

 15 mins   10–15 mins

SERVES 4

INGREDIENTS

9 oz/250 g rice stick noodles

3 tbsp groundnut oil

3 garlic cloves, finely chopped

4½ oz /125 g pork tenderloin, chopped into ¼ inch/5 mm pieces

1¼ cups shrimp, peeled

1 tbsp sugar

3 tbsp Thai fish sauce

1 tbsp tomato ketchup

1 tbsp lime juice

2 eggs, beaten

1 cup beansprouts

TO GARNISH

1 tsp dried red chili flakes

2 scallions, thickly sliced

2 tbsp cilantro, chopped

1 Soak the rice noodles in hot water for about 15 minutes, or according to the package directions. Drain well and put them to one side.

2 Heat the oil in a large, preheated skillet or wok and cook the garlic over a high heat for about 30 seconds. Add the pork, and stir-fry it for 2–3 minutes until the meat is evenly browned.

3 Stir in the shrimp, add the sugar, fish sauce, ketchup, and lime juice, and continue stir-frying for 30 seconds.

4 Stir in the eggs and cook until lightly set. Stir in the noodles, add the beansprouts, and stir-fry for 30 seconds.

5 Serve on a platter scattered with chili flakes, scallions, and cilantro.

COOK'S TIP
Drain the rice noodles thoroughly before adding to the skillet because excess moisture will spoil the texture of the dish.

Rice Noodles & Mushrooms

An alternative to classic noodle dishes such as Pad Thai Noodles, this quick and easy dish contains tofu and is very filling.

NUTRITIONAL INFORMATION

Calories	...361	Sugars	...3g
Protein	...9g	Fat	...12g
Carbohydrate	...53g	Saturates	...2g

15 mins   10 mins

SERVES 4

INGREDIENTS

8 oz/225 g rice stick noodles

2 tbsp vegetable oil

1 garlic clove, finely chopped

¾ inch/2 cm piece fresh ginger root, finely chopped

4 shallots, thinly sliced

¾ cup shiitake mushrooms, sliced

½ cup firm tofu, cut into ⅝ inch/1.5 cm dice

2 tbsp light soy sauce

1 tbsp rice wine

1 tbsp Thai fish sauce

1 tbsp smooth peanut butter

1 tsp chili sauce

2 tbsp toasted peanuts, chopped

shredded basil leaves, to serve

1 Soak the rice stick noodles in hot water for 15 minutes, or according to the package directions. Drain well.

2 Heat the oil in a skillet or wok and stir-fry the garlic, ginger, and shallots for 1–2 minutes until softened and lightly browned.

3 Add the mushrooms to the skillet and stir-fry for an additional 2–3 minutes. Stir in the tofu and toss gently to brown lightly.

4 Mix together the soy sauce, rice wine, fish sauce, peanut butter and chili sauce, then stir into the skillet.

5 Stir in the rice noodles and toss to coat evenly in the sauce. Scatter with the chopped peanuts and shredded basil leaves and serve hot.

COOK'S TIP

Replace the shiitake mushrooms with a can of Chinese straw mushrooms. Alternatively, use dried shiitake mushrooms, soaked and drained before use.

Drunken Noodles

Perhaps this would be more correctly named "drunkards' noodles," because it is supposedly often eaten as a hangover cure.

NUTRITIONAL INFORMATION

Calories	278	Sugars	.........3g
Protein	........12g	Fat	...........7g
Carbohydrate	...40g	Saturates	.......1g

 15 mins   10 mins

SERVES 4

I N G R E D I E N T S

6 oz/175 g rice stick noodles

2 tbsp vegetable oil

1 garlic clove, crushed

2 small green chiles, chopped

1 small onion, thinly sliced

5½ oz/150 g lean ground pork
   or chicken

1 small green bell pepper, deseeded and
   finely chopped

4 kaffir lime leaves, finely shredded

1 tbsp dark soy sauce

1 tbsp light soy sauce

½ tsp sugar

1 tomato, cut into thin wedges

2 tbsp sweet basil leaves, finely sliced,
   to garnish

1 Soak the rice stick noodles in hot water for 15 minutes, or according to the package directions. Drain well.

2 Heat the oil in a wok and stir-fry the garlic, chiles, and onion for 1 minute.

3 Stir in the pork or chicken and stir-fry on a high heat for another minute, then add the bell pepper and continue stir-frying for an additional 2 minutes.

4 Stir in the lime leaves, soy sauces, and sugar. Add the noodles and tomato and toss well to heat thoroughly.

5 Sprinkle the drunken noodles with the sliced basil leaves and serve hot.

COOK'S TIP

Fresh kaffir lime leaves freeze well, simply tie them in a tightly sealed polythene (plastic) freezer bag and freeze for up to a month. They can be used straight from the freezer.

Rice Noodles with Chicken

The great thing about stir-fries is you can use very little fat and still get lots of flavor, as in this light, healthy lunch dish that is low in fat.

NUTRITIONAL INFORMATION

Calories	329	Sugars	. . . . .3g
Protein	. . . . .25g	Fat	. . . . .4g
Carbohydrate	. . .46g	Saturates	. . . . . . .1g

 15 mins   10 mins

SERVES 4

I N G R E D I E N T S

7 oz/200 g rice stick noodles

1 tbsp sunflower oil

1 garlic clove, finely chopped

¾ inch/2 cm piece fresh ginger root, finely chopped

4 scallions, chopped

1 red bird-eye chile, deseeded and sliced

2 cups boneless, skinless chicken, finely chopped

2 chicken livers, finely chopped

1 celery stalk, thinly sliced

1 carrot, cut into fine short thin sticks

5½ cups shredded Napa cabbage

4 tbsp lime juice

2 tbsp Thai fish sauce

1 tbsp soy sauce

TO GARNISH

2 tbsp fresh mint, shredded

slices of pickled garlic

fresh mint sprig

1 Soak the rice noodles in hot water for 15 minutes, or according to the package directions. Drain well.

2 Heat the oil in a wok or large skillet and stir-fry the garlic, ginger, scallions, and chile for about 1 minute. Stir in the chicken and chicken livers, then stir-fry over a high heat for 2–3 minutes until they begin to brown.

3 Stir in the celery and carrot and stir-fry for 2 minutes to soften. Add the Napa cabbage, then stir in the lime juice, fish sauce, and soy sauce.

4 Add the noodles and stir to heat them through thoroughly, then sprinkle them with shredded mint and pickled garlic. Serve immediately, garnished with a fresh sprig of mint.

Stir-fried Pork with Pasta

This delicious dish, with its flavorful hint of Thai cuisine, will certainly get the tastebuds tingling.

NUTRITIONAL INFORMATION

Calories 751	Sugars 10g	
Protein 37g	Fat 27g	
Carbohydrate . . .96g	Saturates 8g	

 20 mins   15 mins

SERVES 4

INGREDIENTS

3 tbsp sesame oil

12 oz/350 g pork tenderloin, cut into thin strips

1 lb/450 g dried taglioni

1 tbsp olive oil

8 shallots, sliced

2 garlic cloves, finely chopped

1 inch/2.5 cm piece ginger root, grated

1 fresh green chile, finely chopped

1 red bell pepper, cored, seeded and thinly sliced

1 green bell pepper, cored, seeded, and thinly sliced

3 zucchini, thinly sliced

2 tbsp ground almonds

1 tsp ground cinnamon

1 tbsp oyster sauce

2 oz/60 g creamed coconut (see Cook's Tip, below), grated

salt and pepper

1 Heat the oil in a wok. Season the pork and stir-fry for 5 minutes.

2 Bring a pan of lightly salted water to a boil. Add the taglioni and olive oil and cook for 12 minutes, until just tender.,Set aside and keep warm.

3 Add the shallots, garlic, ginger, and chile to the wok and stir-fry for 2 minutes. Add the bell peppers and zucchini and stir-fry for 1 minute.

4 Finally, add the ground almonds, cinnamon, oyster sauce and creamed coconut to the wok and stir-fry for 1 minute.

5 Drain the taglioni and transfer to a serving dish. Top with the stir-fry and serve immediately.

COOK'S TIP

Creamed coconut is available from Chinese and Asian food stores and some large supermarkets. It is sold in the form of compressed blocks and adds a concentrated coconut flavor to the dish.

Pad Thai

All over Thailand and Southeast Asia, cooks sell these simple, delicious rice noodles from street stalls and boats, stir-fried to order.

NUTRITIONAL INFORMATION

Calories 527   Sugars 8g
Protein . . . . .34g   Fat 17g
Carbohydrate . . .58g   Saturates 3g

 15 mins   10 mins

SERVES 4

INGREDIENTS

8 oz/225 g flat rice noodles (sen lek)

2 tbsp groundnut or vegetable oil

8 oz/225 g boneless chicken breasts, skinned and thinly sliced

4 shallots, finely chopped

2 garlic cloves, finely chopped

4 scallions, cut on the diagonal into 2 inch/5 cm pieces

12 oz/350 g fresh white crabmeat

1 cup fresh beansprouts, rinsed

1 tbsp preserved radish or fresh radish, finely diced

2–4 tbsp roasted peanuts, chopped

fresh cilantro sprigs, to garnish

SAUCE

3 tbsp Thai fish sauce

2–3 tbsp rice vinegar or cider vinegar

1 tbsp chili bean sauce or oyster sauce

1 tbsp toasted sesame oil

1 tbsp palm sugar or brown sugar

½ tsp cayenne pepper or fresh red chile, thinly sliced

1 To make the sauce, whisk together the sauce ingredients in a small bowl and set aside.

2 Put the rice noodles in a large bowl and pour over enough hot water to cover; let stand for 15 minutes until softened. Drain, rinse, and drain again.

3 Heat the oil in a heavy-based wok over a high heat until very hot, but not smoking. Add the chicken strips and stir-fry for 1–2 minutes until they just begin to color. Using a slotted spoon, transfer to a plate. Reduce the heat to medium-high.

4 Stir the shallots, garlic, and scallions into the wok and stir-fry for about 1 minute. Stir in the drained noodles, then the prepared sauce.

5 Return the reserved chicken to the pan with the crab-meat, beansprouts, and radish; toss well. Cook for about 5 minutes until heated through, tossing frequently. If the noodles begin to stick, add a little water.

6 Turn out onto a serving dish and sprinkle with the chopped roasted peanuts. Garnish with cilantro sprigs and serve immediately.

Stir-Fried Beef

A quick-and-easy stir-fry for any day of the week, this simple beef recipe is a good one-pan main dish. Serve with a simple green side salad.

NUTRITIONAL INFORMATION

Calories	583	Sugars	........13g
Protein	........40g	Fat	..........22g
Carbohydrate	...59g	Saturates	.......7g

 10 mins   15–20 mins

SERVES 4

INGREDIENTS

1 bunch scallions

2 tbsp sunflower oil

1 garlic clove, crushed

1 tsp finely fresh ginger root, chopped

1 lb 2 oz/500 g tender beef, cut into thin strips

1 large red bell pepper, deseeded and sliced

1 small red chili, deseeded and chopped

3⅓ cups fresh beansprouts

1 small lemon grass stem, finely chopped

2 tbsp smooth peanut butter

4 tbsp coconut milk

1 tbsp rice vinegar

1 tbsp soy sauce

1 tsp brown sugar

9 oz/250 g medium egg noodles

salt and pepper

1 Trim and thinly slice the scallions, setting aside some slices to use as a garnish.

2 Heat the oil in a skillet or wok over a high heat. Add the onions, garlic, and ginger and then stir-fry for 2–3 minutes to soften. Add the beef and continue stir-frying for 4–5 minutes until browned evenly.

3 Add the bell pepper and stir-fry for an additional 3–4 minutes. Add the chile and beansprouts and stir-fry for 2 minutes. Mix together the lemon grass, peanut butter, coconut milk, vinegar, soy sauce, and sugar, then stir this mixture into the wok.

4 Meanwhile, cook the egg noodles in boiling, lightly salted water for 4 minutes, or according to the package directions. Drain and stir into the skillet or wok, tossing to mix evenly.

5 Adjust seasoning with salt and pepper to taste. Sprinkle the beef and vegetables with the reserved scallions and serve hot.

Beef Satay

Satay recipes vary throughout the East, but these little beef skewers are a classic version of the traditional dish.

NUTRITIONAL INFORMATION

Calories 489	Sugars 14g
Protein 38g	Fat 31g
Carbohydrate ...17g	Saturates 8g

20 mins   10–15 mins

SERVES 4

INGREDIENTS

1 lb 2 oz/500 g beef tenderloin

2 garlic cloves, crushed

¾ inch/2 cm piece fresh ginger root, finely grated

1 tbsp brown sugar

1 tbsp dark soy sauce

1 tbsp lime juice

2 tsp sesame oil

1 tsp ground coriander

1 tsp turmeric

½ tsp chili powder

chopped cucumber and red bell pepper, to serve

PEANUT SAUCE

1¼ cups coconut milk

8 tbsp crunchy peanut butter

½ small onion, grated

2 tsp brown sugar

½ tsp chilli powder

1 tbsp dark soy sauce

COOK'S TIP

The broiler must be very hot to cook the beef quickly enough to seal it. Soak the skewers in water for 20 minutes before threading them, to reduce the risk of burning.

1 Cut the beef into ½ inch/1 cm cubes and place them in a large bowl.

2 Add the garlic, ginger, sugar, soy sauce, lime juice, sesame oil, ground coriander, turmeric, and chili powder to the bowl. Mix well to coat the pieces of meat evenly with the spices. Cover the bowl and leave the mixture to marinate in the refrigerator for at least 2 hours, or overnight if possible.

3 To make the peanut sauce, place all the ingredients in a pan and stir over a medium heat until boiling. Remove from the heat and keep warm.

4 Thread the beef cubes onto bamboo skewers. Broil the skewers under a preheated broiler for 3–5 minutes, turning often, until golden. Alternatively, barbecue over hot coals. Serve with the sauce and cucumber and bell pepper as garnish.

Beef, Peppers, & Lemon Grass

A delicately flavored stir-fry infused with lemon grass and ginger. Bell peppers add color and it is all cooked within minutes.

NUTRITIONAL INFORMATION

Calories ....230 Sugars 4g
Protein ....26g Fat 12g
Carbohydrate ....6g Saturates 3g

  1–15 mins 10 mins

SERVES 4

I N G R E D I E N T S

1 lb 2 oz/500 g lean beef tenderloin

2 tbsp vegetable oil

1 garlic clove, finely chopped

1 lemon grass stem, finely shredded

1 inch/2.5 cm piece ginger root, finely chopped

1 red bell pepper, deseeded and thickly sliced

1 green bell pepper, deseeded and thickly sliced

1 onion, thickly sliced

2 tbsp lime juice

boiled noodles or rice, to serve

1 Cut the beef into long, thin strips, cutting across the grain.

2 Heat the oil in a large skillet or wok over a high heat. Add the garlic and stir-fry for 1 minute.

3 Add the beef and stir-fry for an additional 2–3 minutes until lightly colored. Stir in the lemon grass and ginger and remove the wok from the heat.

4 Remove the beef from the skillet or wok and keep to one side. Next add the red and green bell peppers and onion to the skillet or wok and stir-fry over a high heat for 2–3 minutes until the onions are just turning golden brown and are softened slightly.

5 Return the beef to the wok, stir in the lime juice, and season to taste with salt and pepper. Serve with noodles or rice.

COOK'S TIP

When preparing lemon grass, take care to remove the outer layers, which can be tough and fibrous. Use only the center, tender part, which has the finest flavor.

Hot Beef & Coconut Curry

The heat of the chiles in this red-hot curry is balanced and softened by coconut milk, producing a creamy-textured and lavishly spiced dish.

NUTRITIONAL INFORMATION

Calories	230	Sugars	.........6g
Protein	........29g	Fat	..........10g
Carbohydrate	....8g	Saturates	.......3g

10–15 mins   30–35 mins

SERVES 4

INGREDIENTS

1¾ cups coconut milk

2 tbsp Thai red curry paste

2 garlic cloves, crushed

1lb 2 oz/500 g braising steak

2 kaffir lime leaves, shredded

3 tbsp kaffir lime juice

2 tbsp Thai fish sauce

1 large red chile, deseeded and sliced

½ tsp turmeric

½ tsp salt

2 tbsp fresh basil leaves, chopped

2 tbsp fresh cilantro leaves, chopped

shredded coconut, to garnish

boiled rice, to serve

1 Place the coconut milk in a pan and bring to a boil. Lower the heat and simmer for about 10 minutes until the milk has thickened. Stir in the curry paste and garlic and simmer for an additional 5 minutes.

2 Cut the beef into ¾ inch/2 cm chunks, add to the pan and bring to a boil, stirring. Lower the heat and add the lime leaves, lime juice, fish sauce, chile, turmeric, and salt.

3 Cover the pan and continue simmering for 20–25 minutes until the meat is tender, adding a little water if the sauce looks too dry.

4 Stir in the basil and cilantro. Sprinkle with coconut and serve with plain rice.

COOK'S TIP

Use a large, mild red chile pepper—a fresno or a Dutch—because they give the dish more color. If you use Thai, or bird-eye, chiles, you need only one because they are much hotter.

Roasted Red Pork

This red-glazed, sweet-and-tender pork, of Chinese origin, is a colorful addition to many stir-fries, salads, and soups.

NUTRITIONAL INFORMATION

Calories	276	Sugars	.........5g
Protein	........34g	Fat	..........13g
Carbohydrate	....7g	Saturates	.......4g

10–15 mins   55–60 mins

SERVES 4

I N G R E D I E N T S

1 lb 5 oz/600 g pork tenderloins

Napa cabbage, shredded to serve

red chile flower, to garnish

M A R I N A D E

2 garlic cloves, crushed

1 tbsp fresh ginger root, grated

1 tbsp light soy sauce

1 tbsp Thai fish sauce

1 tbsp rice wine

1 tbsp hoi-sin sauce

1 tbsp sesame oil

1 tbsp palm sugar or soft brown sugar

½ tsp five-spice powder

a few drops red food coloring (optional)

1 Mix all the ingredients for the marinade together and spread over the pork, turning to coat evenly. Place in a large dish, cover, and put in the refrigerator to marinate overnight.

2 Place a rack in a roasting pan, then half-fill the pan with boiling water. Lift the pork from the marinade and place the meat on the rack. Reserve the marinade for later use.

3 Roast in a preheated oven at 425°F/220°C for about 20 minutes. Baste with the marinade, then lower the heat to 350°F/180°C and continue roasting for an additional 35–40 minutes, basting occasionally, until the pork is a reddish brown and thoroughly cooked.

4 Cut the pork into slices and serve on a bed of shredded Napa cabbage, garnished with a red chile flower.

COOK'S TIP

The pork may also be broiled. Cut the meat into slices or strips and coat in the marinade, then arrange on a tinfoil-lined broiler pan and broil under a high heat, turning occasionally and basting with marinade.

Pork with Sesame Seeds

Thai cooks are fond of adding sweet flavors to meat, as in this unusual pork dish, with soy and garlic to balance the sweetness of the honey.

NUTRITIONAL INFORMATION

Calories 322	Sugars 8g
Protein 35g	Fat 14g
Carbohydrate ...13g	Saturates 4g

 15 mins   40–45 mins

SERVES 4

INGREDIENTS

2 pork tenderloins, about
  9½ oz/275 g each

2 tbsp dark soy sauce

2 tbsp clear honey

2 garlic cloves, crushed

1 tbsp sesame seeds

1 onion, thinly sliced in rings

1 tbsp seasoned all-purpose flour

sunflower oil, to cook

crisp salad, to serve

1 Trim the fat off the pork tenderloins and place them in a wide nonmetallic dish.

2 Mix together the soy sauce, clear honey, and garlic. Spread this mixture over the pork tenderloins, turning the meat to coat it evenly.

3 Lift the pork tenderloin into a roasting pan or shallow ovenproof dish. Sprinkle evenly with the sesame seeds.

4 Roast the pork in an oven preheated at 400°F/200°C for about 20 minutes, spooning over any juices. Cover loosely with tinfoil to prevent overbrowning and roast for an additional 10–15 minutes until the meat is thoroughly cooked.

5 Meanwhile, dip the onion slices in the flour and shake off the excess. Heat the oil and fry the onion rings until golden and crisp, turning occasionally. Serve the pork in slices with the fried onions on a bed of crisp salad.

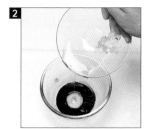

COOK'S TIP

This pork is also excellent served cold, and it's a good choice for picnics, especially served with a spicy sambal or chili relish.

Spicy Fried Ground Pork

A warmly spiced dish, this is ideal for a quick family meal. Just cook fine egg noodles for an accompaniment while the meat sizzles.

NUTRITIONAL INFORMATION

Calories 278	Sugars 4g
Protein 28g	Fat 16g
Carbohydrate 7g	Saturates 4g

 10 mins   15–20 mins

SERVES 4

INGREDIENTS

2 garlic cloves

3 shallots

1 inch/2.5 cm piece fresh ginger root, finely chopped

2 tbsp sunflower oil

1 lb 2 oz/500 g lean ground pork

2 tbsp Thai fish sauce

1 tbsp dark soy sauce

1 tbsp Thai red curry paste

4 dried kaffir lime leaves, crumbled

4 plum tomatoes, chopped

3 tbsp cilantro, chopped

salt and pepper

boiled fine egg noodles, to serve

cilantro sprigs, to garnish

1 Peel and finely chop the garlic, shallots, and ginger. Heat the oil in a wok over a medium heat. Add the garlic, shallots, and ginger and stir-fry for about 2 minutes. Stir in the pork and continue stir-frying until golden brown.

2 Stir in the fish sauce, soy sauce, curry paste, and lime leaves, and stir-fry for an additional 1–2 minutes over a high heat.

3 Add the tomatoes and cook for an additional 5–6 minutes, stirring occasionally.

4 Stir in the chopped cilantro and season to taste with salt and pepper. Serve hot, spooned onto boiled fine egg noodles, garnished with cilantro sprigs.

COOK'S TIP

Dried kaffir lime leaves can be crumbled straight into dishes such as this. Fresh leaves need to be shredded finely before adding.

Red Lamb Curry

This richly spiced curry uses the red-hot chili flavor of Thai red curry paste, made with dried red chilis, to give it a warm, russet-red color.

NUTRITIONAL INFORMATION

Calories	363	Sugars	........11g
Protein	........29g	Fat	..........19g
Carbohydrate	...21g	Saturates	.......6g

15–20 mins   30–35 mins

SERVES 4

INGREDIENTS

1 lb 2 oz/500 g boneless lean leg of lamb

2 tbsp vegetable oil

1 large onion, sliced

2 garlic cloves, crushed

2 tbsp Thai red curry paste

⅔ cup coconut milk

1 tbsp brown sugar

1 large red bell pepper, deseeded and thickly sliced

½ cup lamb or beef bouillon

1 tbsp Thai fish sauce

2 tbsp lime juice

8 oz/227 g canned water chestnuts, drained

2 tbsp fresh cilantro, chopped

2 tbsp fresh basil, chopped

salt and pepper

boiled jasmine rice, to serve

fresh basil leaves, to garnish

COOK'S TIP

This curry can also be made with other lean red meats. Try replacing the lamb with trimmed duck breasts or pieces of lean braising beef.

1 Trim the meat and cut into 1¼ inch/ 3 cm cubes. Heat the oil in a skillet over a high heat and cook the onion and garlic for 2–3 minutes to soften. Add the meat and cook quickly until lightly browned.

2 Stir in the curry paste and cook for a few seconds, then add the coconut milk and sugar and bring to a boil. Reduce the heat and simmer for 15 minutes, stirring occasionally.

3 Stir in the red bell pepper, bouillon, fish sauce, and lime juice, cover, and continue simmering for an additional 15 minutes, or until the meat is tender.

4 Add the water chestnuts, cilantro and basil, adjust the seasoning to taste. Serve with jasmine rice garnished with fresh basil leaves.

Chicken & Mango Stir-Fry

A colorful, exotic mix of flavors that works surprisingly well, this dish is easy and quick to cook—ideal for a mid-week family meal.

NUTRITIONAL INFORMATION

Calories	200	Sugars	.........5g
Protein	........23g	Fat	...........6g
Carbohydrate	....7g	Saturates	.......1g

 15 mins 10–15 mins

SERVES 4

I N G R E D I E N T S

6 boneless, skinless chicken thighs

1 inch/2.5 cm piece fresh ginger root, grated

1 garlic clove, crushed

1 small red chile, deseeded

1 large red bell pepper

4 scallions

1½ cups snow peas

1 cup baby corn cobs

1 large, firm, ripe mango

2 tbsp sunflower oil

1 tbsp light soy sauce

3 tbsp rice wine or sherry

1 tsp sesame oil

salt and pepper

sliced chives, to garnish

1 Cut the chicken into long, thin strips and place them in a bowl. Mix together the ginger, garlic, and chile, then add the mixture to the chicken strips stirring to coat them evenly.

2 Slice the bell pepper thinly, cutting diagonally. Trim and diagonally slice the scallions. Cut the snow peas and corn in half diagonally. Peel the mango, remove the seed, and slice thinly.

3 Heat the sunflower oil in a large skillet or a wok over a high heat. Add the chicken slices and stir-fry them for 4–5 minutes until just they turn golden brown. Add the red bell pepper and stir-fry over a medium heat for 4–5 minutes to soften them.

4 Add the scallions, snow peas, and corncobs, and stir-fry the mixture for an additional minute.

5 Mix together the soy sauce, rice wine or sherry, and the sesame oil, and stir it into the wok. Add the mango and stir gently for 1 minute to heat thoroughly.

6 Adjust the seasoning with salt and pepper to taste, and serve immediately. Garnish with chives.

Thai Coriander Chicken

These simple marinated chicken breasts are packed with powerful, zesty flavors and are best accompanied by a simple dish of plain boiled rice.

NUTRITIONAL INFORMATION

Calories	171	Sugars	.........8g
Protein	........31g	Fat	..........2g
Carbohydrate	....9g	Saturates	.....0.5g

 15 mins   15–20 mins

SERVES 4

INGREDIENTS

4 boneless chicken breasts,
   without skin

2 garlic cloves, peeled

1 fresh green chile, deseeded

¾ inch/2 cm piece fresh ginger root, peeled

4 tbsp fresh cilantro, chopped

rind of 1 lime, finely grated

3 tbsp lime juice

2 tbsp light soy sauce

1 tbsp superfine sugar

¾ cup coconut milk

plain boiled rice, to serve

cucumber and radish slices, to garnish

1 Using a sharp knife, cut 3 deep slashes into the skinned side of each chicken breast. Place the breasts in a single layer in a wide, nonmetallic dish.

2 Put the garlic, chile, ginger, cilantro, lime rind and juice, soy sauce, superfine sugar, and coconut milk in a food processor and process until a smooth purée forms.

3 Spread the purée over both sides of the chicken breasts, coating them evenly. Cover the dish and put it in the refrigerator to marinate for about 1 hour.

4 Lift the chicken from the marinade, drain off the excess and place in a broiler pan. Broil under a preheated broiler for 12–15 minutes until thoroughly and evenly cooked.

5 Meanwhile, place the remaining marinade in a pan and bring to a boil. Lower the heat and simmer for several minutes to heat thoroughly. Serve with the chicken breasts, accompanied with rice and garnished with cucumber and radish slices.

Green Chicken Curry

Thai curries are traditionally very hot and designed to make a little go a long way—the thin, highly spiced juices are eaten with lots of rice.

NUTRITIONAL INFORMATION

Calories 193   Sugars 9g
Protein ....22g   Fat 8g
Carbohydrate ....9g   Saturates 1g

 10 mins   45–50 mins

SERVES 4

INGREDIENTS

6 boneless, skinless chicken thighs, cut into bite-sized pieces

1¾ cups coconut milk

2 garlic cloves, crushed

2 tbsp Thai fish sauce

2 tbsp Thai green curry paste

12 baby eggplants, also called Thai pea eggplants

3 green chiles, finely chopped

3 kaffir lime leaves, shredded

4 tbsp fresh cilantro, chopped

boiled rice, to serve

1 Pour the coconut milk into a large skillet or wok, place over a high heat, and bring to a boil.

2 Add the chicken pieces, garlic, and fish sauce to the skillet and bring back to a boil. Lower the heat and simmer gently for about 30 minutes, or until the chicken is just tender.

3 Remove the chicken from the mixture. Set aside and keep warm.

4 Stir the green curry paste into the skillet, add the eggplants, chiles, and lime leaves and simmer for 5 minutes.

5 Return the chicken to the skillet and bring to a boil. Season to taste with salt and pepper, then stir in the cilantro. Serve the curry with boiled rice.

COOK'S TIP
Baby or 'pea eggplants' as the Thais call them, are traditionally used in this curry. If you cannot find them use chopped ordinary eggplants or substitute green peas.

Glazed Duck Breasts

Duck is excellent cooked with strong flavors, and when it is marinated and coated in this rich, dark, sticky Asian glaze it is irresistible.

NUTRITIONAL INFORMATION

Calories	264	Sugars	.........1g
Protein	........30g	Fat	...........11g
Carbohydrate	...13g	Saturates	.......3g

20 mins   10–15 mins

SERVES 4

I N G R E D I E N T S

4 boneless duck breasts

2 garlic cloves, crushed

4 tsp brown sugar

3 tbsp lime juice

1 tbsp soy sauce

1 tsp chili sauce

1 tsp vegetable oil

2 tbsp plum jam

½ cup chicken bouillon

salt and pepper

1 Using a small, sharp knife, cut deep slashes in the skin of the duck to make a diamond pattern. Place the duck breasts in a wide, nonmetallic dish.

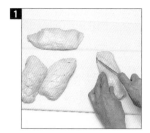

2 Mix together the garlic, sugar, lime juice, soy and chili sauces, then spoon over the duck breasts, turning well to coat them evenly. Cover the dish with plastic wrap and put in the refrigerator to marinate for at least 3 hours, or overnight.

3 Drain the duck, reserving the marinade. Heat a large, heavy-based skillet until very hot and brush with the oil. Add the duck breasts, skin side down, and cook for about 5 minutes or until the skin is browned and crisp. Tip away the excess fat. Turn the duck breasts over.

4 Continue cooking on the other side for 2–3 minutes to brown. Add the reserved marinade, plum jam, and bouillon and simmer for 2 minutes. Adjust the seasoning to taste and serve hot, with the juices spooned over.

COOK'S TIP

If you prefer to reduce the overall fat content of this dish, remove the skin from the duck breasts before cooking and reduce the cooking time slightly.

Crispy Duck with Noodles

A robustly flavored dish that makes a substantial main course. Serve it with a refreshing cucumber salad or a light vegetable stir-fry.

NUTRITIONAL INFORMATION

Calories 433	Sugars 7g	
Protein 25g	Fat 10g	
Carbohydrate ...59g	Saturates 2g	

15 mins   20–25 mins

SERVES 4

INGREDIENTS

3 duck breasts, total weight about 14 oz/400 g

2 garlic cloves, crushed

1½ tsp chili paste

1 tbsp honey

3 tbsp dark soy sauce

½ tsp five-spice powder

9 oz/250 g rice stick noodles

1 tsp vegetable oil

1 tsp sesame oil

2 scallions, sliced

¾ cup snow peas

2 tbsp tamarind juice

sesame seeds, to garnish

1 Prick the duck breast skin all over with a fork and place the duck breasts in a deep dish.

2 Mix together the garlic, chili, honey, soy sauce, and five-spice powder, then pour over the duck. Turn the breasts over to coat them evenly, then cover and put in the refrigerator to marinate for at least 1 hour.

3 Meanwhile, soak the rice noodles in hot water for 15 minutes. Drain well.

4 Drain the duck breasts halves from the marinade and broil on a rack under high heat for about 10 minutes, turning them over occasionally, until they become a rich golden brown. Remove and slice the duck breasts thinly.

5 Heat the vegetable and sesame oils in a skillet and toss the scallions and snow peas for 2 minutes. Stir the reserved marinade and tamarind juice into the mixture, and bring to a boil.

6 Add the sliced duck and noodles to the skillet and toss to heat them through thoroughly. Serve immediately, sprinkled with sesame seeds.

Thai Green Fish Curry

This pale-green curry paste can be used as the basis for a range of Thai dishes. It is also delicious with chicken and beef.

NUTRITIONAL INFORMATION

Calories	217	Sugars	3g
Protein	12g	Fat	17g
Carbohydrate	5g	Saturates	10g

20 mins   15 mins

SERVES 4

INGREDIENTS

2 tbsp vegetable oil

1 garlic clove, chopped

1 small eggplant, diced

½ cup coconut cream

2 tbsp Thai fish sauce

1 tsp sugar

8 oz/225 g firm white fish, cut into pieces, such as cod, haddock, halibut

½ cup fish bouillon

2 lime leaves, finely shredded

about 15 leaves Thai basil, if available, or ordinary basil

plain boiled rice or noodles, to serve

GREEN CURRY PASTE

5 green chiles, deseeded and chopped

2 tsp chopped lemon grass

1 large shallot, chopped

2 garlic cloves, chopped

1 tsp freshly grated ginger or galangal, if available

2 cilantro roots, chopped

½ tsp ground coriander

¼ tsp ground cumin

1 kaffir lime leaf, finely chopped

1 tsp shrimp paste (optional)

½ tsp salt

1 Make the curry paste. Put all the ingredients into a blender and blend to a paste; adding a little water if necessary. Alternatively, pound the ingredients, using a mortar and pestle Set aside.

2 In a skillet or wok, heat the oil until almost smoking and add the garlic. Cook until golden. Add the curry paste and stir-fry a few seconds. Add the eggplant and stir-fry for 4–5 minutes until it is soft.

3 Add the coconut cream. Bring to a boil and stir until the cream thickens and curdles slightly. Add the fish sauce and sugar to the skillet and stir well.

4 Add the fish pieces and bouillon. Simmer for 3–4 minutes, stirring occasionally, until the fish is just tender. Add the lime leaves and basil, and cook for another minute. Remove from the skillet. Serve with plain boiled rice or noodles.

Red Shrimp Curry

Like all Thai curries, this one has as its base a paste of chiles and spices, and a sauce of coconut milk.

NUTRITIONAL INFORMATION

Calories 149   Sugars 4g
Protein ....15g   Fat 7g
Carbohydrate ....6g   Saturates 1g

15–20 mins   15–20 mins

SERVES 4

INGREDIENTS

2 tbsp vegetable oil

1 garlic clove, finely chopped

1 tbsp red curry paste

1 cup coconut milk

2 tbsp Thai fish sauce

1 tsp sugar

12 large raw shrimp, de-veined

2 lime leaves, finely shredded

1 small red chile, deseeded and finely sliced

10 leaves Thai basil, if available, or ordinary basil

RED CURRY PASTE

3 dried long red chiles

½ tsp ground coriander

¼ tsp ground cumin

½ tsp ground black pepper

2 garlic cloves, chopped

2 stems lemon grass, chopped

1 kaffir lime leaf, finely chopped

1 tsp freshly grated ginger root or galangal, if available

1 tsp shrimp paste (optional)

1 Make the red curry paste. Put all the ingredients in a blender and blend to a paste, add a little water if necessary. Alternatively, pound the ingredients in a mortar and pestle. Set aside.

2 Heat the oil in a wok or skillet until almost smoking. Add the garlic and cook until golden. Add 1 tablespoon of the curry paste and cook for another minute. Add half the coconut milk, the fish sauce, and sugar. Stir well. The mixture should thicken slightly.

3 Add the shrimp and simmer for 3–4 minutes until they turn color. Add the remaining coconut milk, the lime leaves, and chile. Cook an additional 2–3 minutes until the shrimp are just tender.

4 Add the basil leaves, stir until wilted, and serve immediately.

Coconut Rice & Monkfish

This is a delicious Thai-influenced recipe of rice cooked in coconut milk, with spicy grilled monkfish and fresh peas.

NUTRITIONAL INFORMATION

Calories	440	Sugars	.........8g
Protein	........22g	Fat	..........14g
Carbohydrate	...60g	Saturates	.......2g

 10–15 mins   35 mins

SERVES 4

I N G R E D I E N T S

1 hot red chile, deseeded and chopped

1 tsp crushed chilli flakes

2 garlic cloves, chopped

2 pinches saffron

3 tbsp coarsely chopped mint leaves

4 tbsp olive oil

2 tbsp lemon juice

12 oz/375 g monkfish fillet, cut into
   bite-size pieces

1 onion, finely chopped

1½ cups long-grain rice

14 oz/400g canned chopped tomatoes

¾ cup coconut milk

½ cup peas

salt and pepper

2 tbsp chopped fresh cilantro, to garnish

1 In a food processor or blender, blend together the fresh and dried chilis, garlic, saffron, mint, olive oil, and lemon juice until finely chopped but not smooth.

2 Put the monkfish into a nonmetallic dish and pour over the spice paste, mixing together well. Set aside for 20 minutes to marinate.

3 Heat a large pan until very hot. Using a slotted spoon, lift the monkfish from the marinade and add in batches to the hot pan. Cook for 3–4 minutes until browned and firm. Remove with a slotted spoon and set aside.

4 Add the onion and remaining marinade to the same pan and cook for 5 minutes until softened and lightly browned. Add the rice and stir until well coated. Add the tomatoes and coconut milk. Bring to a boil, cover, and simmer very gently for 15 minutes. Stir in the peas, season, and arrange the fish over the top. Cover and continue to cook over a very low heat for 5 minutes. Serve garnished with the chopped cilantro.

Steamed Yellow Fish Fillets

Thailand has an abundance of fresh fish, which is an important part of the local diet. Dishes such as these steamed fillets are very popular.

NUTRITIONAL INFORMATION

Calories 165	Sugars 1g	
Protein 23g	Fat 2g	
Carbohydrate ...13g	Saturates 1g	

15–20 mins   12–15 mins

SERVES 4

INGREDIENTS

1 lb 2 oz/500 g firm fish fillets, such as red snapper, sole, or monkfish

1 dried red bird-eye chile

1 small onion, chopped

3 garlic cloves, chopped

2 sprigs fresh cilantro

1 tsp coriander seeds

½ tsp turmeric

½ tsp ground black pepper

1 tbsp Thai fish sauce

2 tbsp coconut milk

1 small egg, beaten

2 tbsp rice flour

red and green chile strips, to garnish

soy sauce, to serve

1 Remove any skin from the fish and cut the fillets diagonally into long ³/₄ inch/2 cm wide strips.

2 Place the dried chili, onion, garlic, cilantro and coriander seeds in a pestle and mortar and grind until it is a smooth paste.

3 Add the turmeric, pepper, fish sauce, coconut milk, and beaten egg, stirring well to mix evenly.

4 Dip the fish strips into the paste mixture, then into the rice flour to coat lightly.

5 Bring the water in the bottom of a steamer to a boil, then arrange the fish strips in the top of the steamer. Cover and steam for about 12–15 minutes until the fish is just firm.

6 Garnish the fish with chile strips and serve with soy sauce and an accompaniment of stir-fried vegetables or salad.

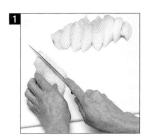

COOK'S TIP

If you don't have a steamer, improvise by placing a large metal colander over a large pan of boiling water and cover with an upturned plate to enclose the fish as it steams.

Baked Fish with Chile Sauce

Almost any whole fish can be cooked by this method, but snapper, sea bass, or tilapia are particularly good with the Thai flavors.

NUTRITIONAL INFORMATION

Calories	267	Sugars	.........9g
Protein	........38g	Fat	...........8g
Carbohydrate	....11g	Saturates	.......2g

10–15 mins   40–45 mins

SERVES 4

I N G R E D I E N T S

handful of fresh sweet basil leaves

1 lb 10 oz/750 g whole red snapper, sea bass, or tilapia, cleaned

2 tbsp peanut oil

2 tbsp Thai fish sauce

2 garlic cloves, crushed

1 tsp galangal or ginger root, finely grated

2 large fresh red chiles, sliced diagonally

1 yellow bell pepper, deseeded and diced

1 tbsp palm sugar

1 tbsp rice vinegar

2 tbsp water or fish stock

2 tomatoes, deseeded and sliced into thin wedges

1 Tuck a few basil leaves inside the body cavity of each fish.

COOK'S TIP

Large red chiles are less hot than the tiny red bird-eye chiles, so you can use them more freely in cooked dishes such as this for a mild heat. Remove the seeds if you prefer.

2 Heat 1 tablespoon oil in a skillet and brown the fish quickly, turning once. Place on tinfoil in a roasting pan and spoon fish sauce over them. Wrap them loosely in the tinfoil, and bake in an oven heated to 375°F/190°C for 25–30 minutes

3 Meanwhile, heat the remaining oil and cook the garlic, galangal, and chiles for 30 seconds. Add the pepper and stir-fry for 2–3 minutes to soften.

4 Stir in the sugar, vinegar, and water, then add the tomatoes and bring to a boil. Remove the pan from the heat.

5 Transfer the fish to a warmed serving plate. Add the fish juices to the pan, then spoon the sauce over the fish and scatter with the reserved basil leaves. Serve immediately.

Curry-Coated Baked Cod

An easy, economical main dish that transforms a piece of white fish into an exotic meal.

NUTRITIONAL INFORMATION

Calories ....223 Sugars 1g
Protein ....31g Fat 4g
Carbohydrate ...16g Saturates 0.1g

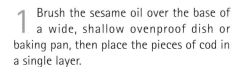 10–15 mins 35–40 mins

SERVES 4

INGREDIENTS

½ tsp sesame oil

4 pieces cod fillet, about 5½ oz/150 g each

1½ cups fresh white bread crumbs

2 tbsp blanched almonds, chopped

2 tsp Thai green curry paste

rind of ½ lime, finely grated

salt and pepper

boiled new potatoes, to serve

lime slices and rind and mixed
green leaves, to garnish

1 Brush the sesame oil over the base of a wide, shallow ovenproof dish or baking pan, then place the pieces of cod in a single layer.

2 Mix the fresh bread crumbs, almonds, curry paste, and lime rind together, stirring well to blend them thoroughly and evenly. Season the mixture to taste with salt and pepper.

3 Carefully spoon the crumb mixture over the fish pieces, pressing lightly to hold it in place.

4 Place the dish, uncovered, in a preheated oven at 400°F/200°C and bake for 35–40 minutes until the fish is cooked through and the crumb topping has cooked to a golden brown.

5 Serve the dish hot, garnished with lime slices and lime rind, and mixed green leaves, and accompanied with boiled new potatoes.

COOK'S TIP
To test whether the fish is cooked through, use a fork to pierce it in the thickest part—if the flesh is white all the way through and flakes apart easily, it is cooked sufficiently.

Sweet & Sour Tuna

Tuna is a firm, meaty-textured fish that is abundant in the seas around Thailand. You can also use shark or mackerel in this dish.

NUTRITIONAL INFORMATION

Calories	303	Sugars	........12g
Protein	........31g	Fat	..........12g
Carbohydrate	...20g	Saturates	.......3g

  10 mins   15–20 mins

SERVES 4

INGREDIENTS

4 fresh tuna steaks, about 1 lb 2 oz/500 g total weight

¼ tsp ground black pepper

2 tbsp peanut oil

1 onion, diced

1 small red bell pepper, deseeded and cut into short thin sticks

1 garlic clove, crushed

½ cucumber, deseeded and cut into short thin sticks

2 pineapple slices, diced

1 tsp fresh ginger root, finely chopped

1 tbsp brown sugar

1 tbsp cornstarch

1½ tbsp lime juice

1 tbsp Thai fish sauce

1 cup fish stock

lime and cucumber slices, to garnish

1 Sprinkle the tuna steaks with pepper on both sides. Heat a heavy skillet or griddle and brush with a little of the oil. Arrange the tuna on the griddle and cook for about 8 minutes, turning them over once.

2 Heat the remaining oil in another skillet and cook the onion, bell pepper, and garlic gently for 3–4 minutes to soften.

3 Remove from the heat and stir in the cucumber, pineapple, ginger, and sugar.

4 Blend the cornstarch with the lime juice and fish sauce, then stir into the stock and add to the skillet. Stir over a medium heat until boiling, then cook for 1–2 minutes until thickened and clear.

5 Spoon the sauce over the tuna and serve garnished with lime slices and cucumber.

COOK'S TIP

Tuna can be served quite lightly cooked; it can be dry if it becomes too overcooked.

Thai-Spiced Salmon

Marinated in delicate Thai spices and quickly pan-fried to perfection, these salmon fillets are ideal for a special dinner.

NUTRITIONAL INFORMATION

Calories 329   Sugars 0.1g
Protein ....30g   Fat 23g
Carbohydrate ...0.1g Saturates 4g

  10 mins   4–5 mins

SERVES 4

I N G R E D I E N T S

1 in/2.5 cm piece fresh ginger root, grated

1 tsp coriander seeds, crushed

¼ tsp chili powder

1 tbsp lime juice

1 tsp sesame oil

4 pieces salmon fillet with skin, about
  5½ oz/150 g each

2 tbsp vegetable oil

boiled rice and stir-fried vegetables,
  to serve

1 Mix together the grated ginger, crushed coriander, chili powder, lime juice, and sesame oil.

2 Place the salmon on a wide, nonmetallic plate or dish and spoon the mixture over the flesh side of the fillets, spreading it to coat each piece of salmon evenly.

3 Cover the dish with plastic wrap and chill the salmon in the refrigerator for 30 minutes.

4 Heat a wide, heavy-based skillet or griddle pan with the oil over a high heat. Place the salmon on the hot skillet or griddle, skin side down.

5 Cook the salmon for 4–5 minutes, without turning, until the salmon is crusty underneath and the flesh flakes easily. Serve at once with the boiled rice and stir-fried vegetables.

COOK'S TIP

It is important to use a heavy-based skillet or a solid griddle for this recipe, so the fish cooks evenly without sticking. Turn a very thick fish carefully to cook on the other side for 2–3 minutes.

Salmon with Red Curry

Banana leaves are widely used in Thai cooking to wrap raw ingredients such as fish before baking or steaming.

1 Place a salmon steak on the center of each half banana leaf.

2 Mix the garlic, ginger, curry paste, sugar, and fish sauce. Spread over the fish and sprinkle with lime juice.

3 Wrap the banana leaves round the fish, tucking in the sides.

4 Place the parcels seam side down on a cookie sheet and bake in an oven preheated to 425°F/220°C for 15–20 minutes until the fish is cooked. Serve garnished with lime wedges and chile.

NUTRITIONAL INFORMATION

Calories 351   Sugars 6g
Protein . . . . .36g   Fat 20g
Carbohydrate . . . .6g   Saturates 3g

15 mins   15–20 mins

SERVES 4

I N G R E D I E N T S

4 salmon steaks, about 6 oz/175 g each

2 banana leaves, halved

1 garlic clove, crushed

1 tsp fresh ginger root, grated

1 tbsp Thai red curry paste

1 tsp brown sugar

1 tbsp Thai fish sauce

2 tbsp lime juice

TO GARNISH

lime wedges

finely chopped red chile

COOK'S TIP

Fresh banana leaves are often sold in packages containing several leaves, but if you buy more than you need, they will store in the refrigerator for about a week.

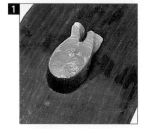

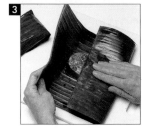

Squid with Hot Sauce

Quick stir-frying is ideal for squid, because if overcooked it can be tough. The technique also seals in the natural colors and flavors.

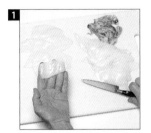

NUTRITIONAL INFORMATION

Calories	245	Sugars 7g
Protein	........32g	Fat 7g
Carbohydrate	...13g	Saturates 1g

 15 mins 5–10 mins

SERVES 4

INGREDIENTS

1 lb 10 oz/750 g squid, cleaned

1 large red bell pepper, deseeded

1 cup snow peas, trimmed

1 head bok choy

3 tbsp black bean sauce

1 tbsp Thai fish sauce

1 tbsp rice wine

1 tbsp dark soy sauce

1 tsp brown sugar

1 tsp cornstarch

1 tbsp water

1 tbsp sunflower oil

1 tsp sesame oil

1 small red bird-eye chile, chopped

1 garlic clove, finely chopped

1 tsp fresh ginger root, grated

2 scallions, chopped

1 Cut the tentacles from the squid and discard. Cut the body cavities into quarters lengthwise. Use the tip of a small sharp knife to score a diamond pattern into the flesh, without cutting all the way through. Pat dry with paper towels.

2 Cut the bell pepper into long, thin slices. Cut the snow peas in half diagonally. Coarsely shred the bok choy.

3 Mix together the black bean sauce, fish sauce, rice wine, soy sauce, and sugar. Blend the cornstarch with the water and stir into the other sauce ingredients. Keep to one side.

4 Heat the sunflower oil and sesame oil in a wok. Add the chile, garlic, ginger, and scallions and stir-fry for about 1 minute. Add the bell pepper and stir-fry for about 2 minutes.

5 Add the squid and stir-fry over a high heat for a further minute. Stir in the snowpeas and bok choy, and stir-fry for a further minute until wilted.

6 Stir in the sauce ingredients and cook, stirring constantly, for about 2 minutes, until the sauce clears and thickens. Serve immediately.

Scallops with Lime & Chile

Really fresh scallops have a delicate flavor and texture, needing only minimal cooking, as in this simple stir-fry.

NUTRITIONAL INFORMATION

Calories ....145 Sugars 1g
Protein ....17g Fat 7g
Carbohydrate ....4g Saturates 3g

🍲 15 mins   🕐 7–8 mins

SERVES 4

INGREDIENTS

16 large scallops

1 tbsp butter

1 tbsp vegetable oil

1 tsp garlic, crushed

1 tsp fresh ginger root, grated

1 bunch scallions, finely sliced

rind of 1 kaffir lime, finely grated

1 small red chile, deseeded and very finely chopped

3 tbsp kaffir lime juice

salt and pepper

lime wedges and boiled rice, to serve

1 Trim the scallops to remove any black intestine. Wash and pat dry. Separate the corals from the white parts. Slice each white part in half, making 2 circles.

2 Heat the butter and oil in a skillet or a wok. Add the garlic and ginger, and stir-fry for 1 minute without browning. Add the scallions and stir-fry for a minute.

3 Add the scallops to the skillet or wok and continue stir-frying over a high heat for 4–5 minutes. Stir in the lime rind, chile. and lime juice and cook for another minute.

4 Serve the scallops hot, with the juices spooned over them, accompanied by lime wedges and boiled rice.

COOK'S TIP

If fresh scallops are not available, frozen ones can be used, but make sure they are thoroughly defrosted before you cook them. Drain off all excess moisture and pat the scallops dry with paper towels.

Spicy Shrimp Skewers

Whole jumbo shrimp cook very quickly on a barbecue or under a broiler so they are ideal for summertime cooking, indoors or outside.

NUTRITIONAL INFORMATION

Calories . . . . .106 Sugars 8g
Protein . . . . .11g Fat 3g
Carbohydrate . . . .8g Saturates 1g

 15–20 mins 5–6 mins

SERVES 4

INGREDIENTS

1 garlic clove, chopped

1 red bird-eye chile, deseeded and chopped

1 tbsp tamarind paste

1 tbsp sesame oil

1 tbsp dark soy sauce

2 tbsp lime juice

1 tbsp brown sugar

16 large whole jumbo shrimp

crusty bread, lime wedges, and salad greens, to serve

1 Put the garlic, chile, tamarind paste, sesame oil, soy sauce, lime juice, and sugar in a small pan. Stir over a low heat until the sugar is dissolved, then remove from the heat and allow to cool completely.

2 Wash and dry the shrimp and place it in one layer in a wide, nonmetal dish. Spoon the marinade over the shrimp and turn them to coat evenly. Cover the dish and put in the refrigerator to marinate for at least 2 hours, or preferably overnight.

3 Meanwhile, soak 4 bamboo or wooden skewers in water for about 20 minutes. Drain and thread 4 shrimp onto each skewer.

4 Broil the skewers under a preheated hot broiler for 5–6 minutes, turning them over once, until they turn pink and begin to brown. Alternatively, you can barbecue the shrimp skewers over hot coals.

5 Thread a wedge of lime onto the end of each skewer and serve with crusty bread and salad greens.

Thai Potato Stir-Fry

This vegetable dish has a traditional sweet-and-sour Thai flavoring. Tender vegetables are stir-fried with spices and coconut milk.

NUTRITIONAL INFORMATION

Calories	138	Sugars	.........5g
Protein	.........2g	Fat	...........6g
Carbohydrate	....1g	Saturates	.......1g

15–20 mins   15 mins

SERVES 4

I N G R E D I E N T S

4 waxy potatoes, diced

2 tbsp vegetable oil

1 yellow bell pepper, diced

1 red bell pepper, diced

1 carrot, cut into short thin sticks

1 zucchini, cut into short thin sticks

2 garlic cloves, crushed

1 red chile, sliced

1 bunch scallions, halved lengthwise

8 tbsp coconut milk

1 tsp chopped lemon grass

2 tsp lime juice

finely grated rind of 1 lime

1 tbsp chopped cilantro

1 Cook the diced potatoes in a pan of boiling water for 5 minutes. Drain the potatoes thoroughly.

2 Heat the oil in a wok or a large skillet and add the potatoes, bell peppers, carrot, zucchini, garlic, and chile. Stir-fry the vegetables for 2–3 minutes.

3 Stir the scallions, coconut milk, chopped lemon grass, and lime juice into the mixture, and stir-fry the vegetables for an additional 5 minutes.

4 Add the lime rind and cilantro and stir-fry for 1 minute. Serve right away, while the vegetables are still hot.

COOK'S TIP

Check that the potatoes are not overcooked in step 1, otherwise the potato pieces will disintegrate when they are stir-fried in the wok.

Thai-Style Caesar Salad

This simple salad uses fried rice paper wrappers as crispy croûtons.
The Thai fish sauce gives the dressing an unusual flavor.

NUTRITIONAL INFORMATION

Calories 533   Sugars 7g
Protein . . . . .4g   Fat 43g
Carbohydrate . . .35g   Saturates 5g

10–15 mins   2–5 mins

SERVES 4

INGREDIENTS

1 large head romaine lettuce, with outer leaves removed, or 2 hearts

vegetable oil, for deep frying

4–6 large rice paper wrappers or 4 oz/120 g rice paper flakes

small bunch of cilantro, leaves stripped from stems

DRESSING

⅓ cup rice vinegar

2–3 tbsp Thai fish sauce

2 garlic cloves, coarsely chopped

1 tbsp sugar

1 inch/2.5 cm piece fresh ginger root, peeled and coarsely chopped

½ cup sunflower oil

salt and pepper

1 Tear the lettuce leaves into bite-size pieces and put in a large salad bowl.

2 To make the salad dressing, put the rice vinegar, fish sauce, garlic, sugar, and ginger in a food processor and process for 15–30 seconds.

3 With the machine running, gradually pour in the sunflower oil until a creamy liquid forms. Season with salt and

pepper to taste and pour the dressing into a pitcher; set aside.

4 Heat about 3 inches/7.5 cm of vegetable oil in a deep-fat fryer to 375°F/190°C.

5 Meanwhile, break the rice wrappers into bite-size pieces and dip each into a bowl of water to soften. Lay on a clean dish cloth and pat completely dry.

6 Working in batches, add the rice paper pieces to the hot oil and cook for about 15 seconds until crisp and golden. Using a slotted spoon, transfer to paper towels to drain.

7 Add the cilantro leaves to the lettuce and toss to mix. Add the fried rice paper "crisps" and drizzle over the dressing. Toss to coat the salad leaves and serve immediately.

Thai Noodle & Shrimp Salad

This composition of rice noodles and shrimp, lightly dressed with Thai flavors, makes an impressive first course or a light lunch.

NUTRITIONAL INFORMATION

Calories	204	Sugars	.........8g
Protein	........15g	Fat	...........3g
Carbohydrate	...29g	Saturates	.......1g

  10–15 mins   5 mins

SERVES 4

I N G R E D I E N T S

3 oz/80 g rice vermicelli or rice sticks

6 oz/175 g snow peas, cut crosswise in half, if large

5 tbsp lime juice

4 tbsp Thai fish sauce

1 tbsp sugar, or to taste

1 inch/2.5 cm piece fresh ginger root, peeled and finely chopped

1 fresh red chile, deseeded and thinly sliced on the diagonal

4 tbsp chopped cilantro or mint, plus extra for garnishing

4 inch/10 cm piece of cucumber, peeled, deseeded and diced

2 scallions, thinly sliced on the diagonal

20–24 large cooked, peeled shrimp

2 tbsp chopped unsalted peanuts (optional)

lemon slices, to garnish

1 Put the rice noodles into a large bowl and pour over them enough hot water to cover. Stand for about 4 minutes until they are soft. Drain and rinse under cold running water; drain and set aside.

2 Bring a pan of water to a boil. Add the snow peas and return to a boil. Simmer for 1 minute. Drain, rinse the snow peas under cold running water until cold, then drain and set aside.

3 In a large bowl, whisk together the lime juice, fish sauce, sugar, ginger, chile and cilantro. Stir in the cucumber and scallions. Add the drained noodles and snow peas. Reserve 4 shrimp and add the rest to the mixture, then toss the salad gently.

4 Divide the noodle salad between 4 large plates. Sprinkle with chopped cilantro and the peanuts (if using), then garnish each plate with a whole shrimp and a lemon slice. Serve immediately.

COOK'S TIP

There are many sizes of rice noodle available—use the very thin rice noodles, called rice vermicelli or rice sticks or sen mee, otherwise the salad will be too heavy.

Thai Seafood Salad

This delicious seafood salad, which includes mussels, shrimp, and squid with light green vegetables, is best served chilled.

NUTRITIONAL INFORMATION

Calories 310   Sugars 4g
Protein . . . . .30g   Fat 18g
Carbohydrate . . . .7g   Saturates 3g

 20 mins, plus chilling   🕑 10–15 mins

SERVES 4

I N G R E D I E N T S

1 lb/450 g live mussels

8 raw jumbo shrimp

12 oz/350 g squid, cleaned and sliced widthwise into rings

4 oz/115 g cooked peeled shrimp

½ red onion, finely sliced

½ red bell pepper, deseeded and sliced finely

1 cup bean-sprouts

2 cups shredded bok choy

D R E S S I N G

1 garlic clove, crushed

1 tsp grated fresh ginger root

1 red chile, deseeded and finely chopped

2 tbsp chopped cilantro

1 tbsp lime juice

1 tsp finely grated lime rind

1 tbsp light soy sauce

5 tbsp sunflower or groundnut oil

2 tsp sesame oil

salt and pepper

1 Scrub the mussel shells and remove any beards. Place in a pan with just the water that clings to the shells. Cook over a high heat for 3–4 minutes, shaking occasionally, until all the mussels have opened. Discard any that remain closed. Strain, reserving the poaching liquid, and refresh the mussels under cold water. Drain and set aside.

2 Bring the reserved poaching liquid to a boil and add the shrimp. Simmer for 5 minutes. Add the squid and cook for 2 minutes. When both are cooked through, remove them, plunge into cold water, and drain. Reserve the liquid.

3 Remove the mussels from their shells and put into a bowl with the jumbo shrimp, squid, and cooked peeled shrimp. Refrigerate for 1 hour.

4 For the dressing, put all the ingredients, except the oils, into a blender and blend to a smooth paste. Add the oils, reserved poaching liquid, seasoning, and 4 tablespoons of cold water. Blend again to combine.

5 Combine the onion, bell pepper, beansprouts, and bok choy in a bowl and toss with 2–3 tablespoons of the dressing. Arrange the vegetables on a large serving plate or in a bowl. Toss the remaining dressing with the seafood to coat and add to the vegetables. Serve at once.

Warm Tuna Salad

A colorful, refreshing first course which is perfect to make for a special summer lunch or dinner. The dressing can be made in advance.

NUTRITIONAL INFORMATION

Calories	127	Sugars	.........4g
Protein	........13g	Fat	...........5g
Carbohydrate	....6g	Saturates	.......1g

 20 mins 10–15 mins

SERVES 4

I N G R E D I E N T S

½ cup Napa cabbage, shredded

3 tbsp rice wine

2 tbsp Thai fish sauce

1 tbsp fresh ginger root, finely shredded

1 garlic clove, finely chopped

½ small red bird-eye chile, finely chopped

2 tsp brown sugar

2 tbsp lime juice

14 oz/400 g fresh tuna steak

sunflower oil for brushing

1 cup cherry tomatoes

fresh mint leaves and mint sprigs, coarsely chopped, to garnish

1 Place some shredded Napa cabbage on a plate. Put the wine, fish sauce, ginger, garlic, chile, sugar, and 1 tablespoon of lime juice in a screw-top jar and shake.

2 Cut the tuna into evenly thick strips. Sprinkle with the remaining lime juice.

3 Brush a skillet or a griddle with the oil and heat until very hot. Arrange the tuna in the skillet, cook until firm and lightly golden, turning over once. Remove the tuna and set it aside.

4 Cook the tomatoes in the skillet over a high heat until lightly browned. Spoon the tuna and tomatoes over the Napa cabbage and spoon over the dressing. Garnish with fresh mint and serve warm.

COOK'S TIP

You can make a quick version of this dish using canned tuna. Just drain and flake the tuna, omit steps 2 and 3 and continue as in the recipe.

Egg Noodle & Turkey Salad

A good dish for summer eating, this is light and refreshing, and easy to cook. The turkey can be replaced with cooked chicken.

NUTRITIONAL INFORMATION

Calories	355	Sugars	.........6g
Protein	........22g	Fat	..........10g
Carbohydrate	...46g	Saturates	.......2g

   15–20 mins   5 mins

SERVES 4

INGREDIENTS

8 oz/225 g dried egg noodles

2 tsp sesame oil

1 carrot

1 cup beansprouts

½ cucumber

5½ oz/150 g cooked turkey breast meat, shredded into thin slivers

2 scallions, finely shredded

peanuts and basil leaves chopped, to garnish

DRESSING

5 tbsp coconut milk

3 tbsp lime juice

1 tbsp light soy sauce

2 tsp Thai fish sauce

1 tsp chili oil

1 tsp sugar

2 tbsp cilantro, chopped

2 tbsp sweet basil, chopped

1 Cook the noodles in boiling water for 4 minutes, or according to the package directions. Plunge them into a bowl of cold water to cool, then drain and toss them in sesame oil.

2 Use a vegetable peeler to shave off thin ribbons from the carrot. Blanch the ribbons and beansprouts in boiling water for 30 seconds, then plunge into cold water for 30 seconds. Drain well. Next, shave thin ribbons of cucumber with the peeler.

3 Toss the carrots, beansprouts, cucumber, and scallions together with the turkey and noodles.

4 Place all of the dressing ingredients in a screw-top jar and shake well to combine them evenly.

5 Add the dressing to the noodle mixture. and toss. Pile onto a serving dish. Sprinkle with peanuts and basil leaves, and serve cold.

Jasmine Rice with Lemon

Jasmine rice has a delicate scent and it can be served completely plain, with no other flavorings. This simple dish has a light tang of lemon.

NUTRITIONAL INFORMATION

Calories	384	Sugars	.........0g
Protein	.........7g	Fat	...........4g
Carbohydrate	...86g	Saturates	.......1g

 5 mins   ⏱ 20-25 mins

SERVES 4

I N G R E D I E N T S

2 cups jasmine rice

3½ cups water

rind of ½ lemon, finely grated

2 tbsp fresh sweet basil, chopped

1 Wash the rice in several changes of cold water until the water runs clear. Bring the water to a boil in a large pan, then add the rice.

2 Bring the water back to a rolling boil. Turn the heat to a low simmer, cover the pan and simmer for an additional 12 minutes.

3 Remove the pan from the heat and let stand, covered, for about 10 minutes.

4 Fluff up the rice with a fork, then stir in the lemon. Serve scattered with basil.

COOK'S TIP

It is important to leave the pan tightly covered while the rice cooks and steams inside so that the grains cook evenly and become fluffy and separate.

Coconut Rice with Pineapple

Cooking rice in coconut milk, as in this dessert, makes it very satisfying and nutritious. This method is often used as a base for main dishes.

NUTRITIONAL INFORMATION

Calories 278	Sugars 11g
Protein 5g	Fat 7g
Carbohydrate ...54g	Saturates 5g

10 mins   20-25 mins

SERVES 4

I N G R E D I E N T S

1 cup long-grain rice

2¼ cups coconut milk

2 lemon grass stems

1 cup water

2 slices fresh pineapple, peeled and diced

2 tbsp toasted coconut

chili sauce, to serve

1 Wash the rice in several changes of cold water until the water runs clear. Place in a large pan with the coconut milk.

2 Place the lemon grass on a firm work surface and bruise it by hitting firmly with a rolling pin or meat hammer. Add to the pan with the rice and coconut milk.

3 Add the water and bring to a boil. Lower the heat, cover the pan tightly, and simmer gently for 15 minutes. Remove the pan from the heat and fluff up the rice with a fork.

4 Remove the lemon grass and stir in the pineapple. Scatter the toasted coconut over the top of the rice and serve with chili sauce.

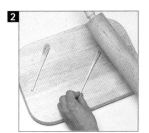

VARIATION

A sweet version of this dish can be made by simply omitting the lemon grass and stirring in palm sugar or caster sugar to taste during cooking. Serve as a dessert, with extra pineapple slices.

Vegetables in Peanut Sauce

This colorful mix of vegetables in a rich, spicy peanut sauce can be served either as a side dish or as a vegetarian main course.

NUTRITIONAL INFORMATION

Calories ....249 Sugars 10g
Protein ....10g Fat 17g
Carbohydrate ...12g Saturates 3g

 15–20 mins   10 mins

SERVES 4

INGREDIENTS

2 carrots, peeled

1 small head cauliflower, trimmed

2 small heads green bok choy

5½ oz/150 g green beans, trimmed, if wished

2 tbsp vegetable oil

1 garlic clove, finely chopped

6 scallions, sliced

1 tsp chili paste

2 tbsp soy sauce

2 tbsp rice wine

4 tbsp smooth peanut butter

3 tbsp coconut milk

COOK'S TIP

It's important to cut the vegetables thinly into even-size pieces so that they cook quickly and evenly. Prepare all the vegetables before you start to cook.

1 Cut the carrots diagonally into thin slices. Cut the cauliflower into small florets, then slice the stem thinly. Thickly slice the bok choy. Cut the beans into 1¼ inch/3 cm lengths.

2 Heat the vegetable oil in a large skillet or wok, and stir-fry the garlic and scallions for about 1 minute, then stir the chili paste into the mixture and cook for a few seconds.

3 Add the carrots and cauliflower, and stir-fry for 2–3 minutes.

4 Add the bok choy and beans, and stir-fry for an additional 2 minutes. Stir in the soy sauce and rice wine.

5 Mix the peanut butter with the coconut milk and stir into the pan, then cook, stirring, for another minute. Serve immediately while still hot.

Thai Red Bean Curry

The "red" in the title refers not to the beans, but to the sauce, which has a warm, rusty red color. This is a good way to serve fresh beans.

NUTRITIONAL INFORMATION

Calories	89	Sugars	.........4g
Protein	.........2g	Fat	...........7g
Carbohydrate	....5g	Saturates	.......1g

 10-15 mins 15 mins

SERVES 4

INGREDIENTS

14 oz/400 g green beans

1 garlic clove, finely sliced

1 red bird-eye chile, deseeded and chopped

½ tsp paprika pepper

1 piece lemon grass stem, finely chopped

2 tsp Thai fish sauce

½ cup coconut milk

1 tbsp sunflower oil

2 scallions, sliced

1 Cut the beans into 2 inch/5 cm pieces and cook in boiling water for about 2 minutes. Drain well.

2 Place the garlic, chile, paprika, lemon grass, fish sauce, and coconut milk in a blender and process until a smooth paste forms.

3 Heat the oil in a skillet and stir-fry the scallions over a high heat for about 1 minute. Add the paste and bring the mixture to a boil.

4 Simmer for 3–4 minutes to reduce the liquid by about half. Add the beans and simmer for an additional 1–2 minutes until tender. Serve hot.

COOK'S TIP
Young string beans can be used instead of green beans. Remove any strings from the beans, then cut at a diagonal angle in short lengths. Cook as the recipe until tender.

Stir-Fried Vegetables

Serve this colorful mixture with a pile of golden, crispy noodles as a vegetarian main course, or on its own to accompany meat dishes.

NUTRITIONAL INFORMATION

Calories ....148 Sugars 7g
Protein ....8g Fat 7g
Carbohydrate ...14g Saturates 1g

   20 mins    10–15 mins

SERVES 4

I N G R E D I E N T S

1 eggplant

salt

2 tbsp vegetable oil

3 garlic cloves, crushed

4 scallions, chopped

1 small red bell pepper, deseeded and thinly sliced

4 baby corncobs, halved lengthwise

1 cup snow peas

2 cups Chinese mustard greens, coarsely shredded

14½ oz/425 g canned Chinese straw mushrooms, drained

1 cup beansprouts

2 tbsp rice wine

2 tbsp yellow bean sauce

2 tbsp dark soy sauce

1 tsp chili sauce

1 tsp sugar

½ cup chicken or vegetable stock

1 tsp cornstarch

2 tsp water

1 Trim the eggplant and cut into 2 inch/5 cm long sticks. Place in a colander, sprinkle with salt, and let drain for 30 minutes. Rinse in cold water and pat dry with paper towels.

2 Heat the oil in a skillet or wok and stir-fry the garlic, scallions, and bell pepper over a high heat for 1 minute. Stir in the eggplant and stir-fry for another minute, or until softened.

3 Stir in the corn and snow peas and stir-fry for about 1 minute. Add the mustard greens, mushrooms, and beansprouts and stir-fry for 30 seconds.

4 Mix together the rice wine, yellow bean sauce, soy sauce, chili sauce, and sugar and add to the skillet with the stock. Bring to a boil, stirring.

5 Slowly blend the cornstarch with the water to form a smooth paste. Stir the paste quickly into the skillet or wok and cook for another minute. Serve the stir-fry immediately.

Broccoli in Oyster Sauce

Chinese oyster sauce has a sweet-salty flavor, ideal for adding a richly Asian flavor to plain vegetables. Try this recipe with fresh asparagus.

NUTRITIONAL INFORMATION

Calories 81   Sugars 2g
Protein . . . . .5g   Fat 4g
Carbohydrate . . . .6g   Saturates 1g

 15 mins   5–10 mins

SERVES 4

INGREDIENTS

14 oz/400 g broccoli

1 tbsp peanut oil

2 shallots, finely chopped

1 garlic clove, finely chopped

1 tbsp rice wine or sherry

5 tbsp oyster sauce

¼ tsp ground black pepper

1 tsp chili oil

1 Trim the broccoli and cut into small florets. Blanch in a pan of boiling water for about 30 seconds, then drain well.

2 Heat the oil in a large skillet or wok and stir-fry the shallots and garlic for about 1–2 minutes until golden brown.

3 Stir in the broccoli florets and stir-fry for 2 minutes. Add the rice wine or sherry and oyster sauce and stir-fry for another 1 minute.

4 Stir in the pepper and drizzle with a little chili oil just before serving.

COOK'S TIP
To make chili oil, tuck red or green chiles into a jar and top up with olive oil or a light vegetable oil. Cover with a lid and set aside to let the flavour infuse for at least 3 weeks before using.

Spiced Cashew Nut Curry

This unusual vegetarian dish is best served as a side dish with vegetable or meat, and rice to soak up the juices.

NUTRITIONAL INFORMATION

Calories	455	Sugars	.........6g
Protein	........13g	Fat	..........39g
Carbohydrate	...16g	Saturates	......11g

10–15 mins   25–30 mins

SERVES 4

INGREDIENTS

1½ cups unsalted cashew nuts

1 tsp coriander seeds

1 tsp cumin seeds

2 cardamom pods, crushed

1 tbsp sunflower oil

1 onion, finely sliced

1 garlic clove, crushed

1 small green chile, deseeded and chopped

1 cinnamon stick

½ tsp ground turmeric

4 tbsp coconut cream

1¼ cups hot vegetable stock

3 kaffir lime leaves, finely shredded

salt and pepper

boiled jasmine rice, to serve

1 Soak the cashew nuts in cold water overnight. Drain thoroughly. Crush the coriander, cumin seeds, and cardamom pods in a pestle and mortar.

2 Heat the oil and stir-fry the onion and garlic for 2–3 minutes to soften, but not brown. Add the chile, crushed spices, cinnamon stick, and turmeric, and stir-fry for another minute.

3 Add the coconut cream and the stock to the pan. Bring to a boil, then add the cashew nuts and lime leaves.

4 Cover the pan, lower the heat, and simmer for about 20 minutes. Serve hot, accompanied by jasmine rice.

COOK'S TIP

All spices give the best flavor when freshly crushed, but if you prefer, you can use ground spices instead of crushing them yourself in a pestle and mortar.

Potato & Spinach Curry

Potatoes are not highly regarded in Thai cooking, since rice is the traditional staple. This dish is a tasty exception.

NUTRITIONAL INFORMATION

Calories 160	Sugars 4g
Protein 3g	Fat 10g
Carbohydrate ...15g	Saturates 1g

10–15 mins   20–25 mins

SERVES 4

I N G R E D I E N T S

2 garlic cloves, finely chopped

1¼ inch/3 cm piece galangal, finely chopped

1 lemon grass stem, finely chopped

1 tsp coriander seeds

3 tbsp vegetable oil

2 tsp Thai red curry paste

½ tsp turmeric

1 cup coconut milk

9 oz/250 g potatoes, peeled and cut into ¾ inch/2 cm cubes

½ cup vegetable stock

3 cups young spinach leaves

1 small onion, thinly sliced into rings

1 Place the garlic, galangal, lemon grass, and coriander seeds in a pestle and mortar and pound until a smooth paste forms.

2 Heat 2 tablespoons of the oil in a skillet or wok. Stir in the paste and stir-fry for 30 seconds. Stir in the curry paste and turmeric, then add the coconut milk and bring to a boil.

3 Add the potatoes and stock. Return to a boil, then lower the heat and simmer, uncovered, for 10–12 minutes until the potatoes are almost tender.

4 Stir in the spinach and simmer until the leaves are just wilted.

5 Meanwhile, cook the onions in the remaining oil until crisp and golden brown. Place on top of the curry just before serving.

COOK'S TIP

Choose a firm, waxy potato for this dish, one that will keep its shape during cooking in preference to a floury variety which will break up easily once cooked.

Crispy Tofu with Chile Sauce

Tempting golden cubes of fried tofu, with colorful carrots and peppers, are combined with a warm chile sauce make an unusual side dish.

NUTRITIONAL INFORMATION

Calories	149	Sugars	.........9g
Protein	.........8g	Fat	...........9g
Carbohydrate	...10g	Saturates	.......1g

 20 mins   10–15 mins

SERVES 4

INGREDIENTS

10½ oz/300 g firm tofu

2 tbsp vegetable oil

1 garlic clove, sliced

1 carrot, cut into short thin sticks

½ green bell pepper, deseeded and cut into short thin sticks

1 red bird-eye chile, deseeded and finely chopped

2 tbsp soy sauce

1 tbsp lime juice

1 tbsp Thai fish sauce

1 tbsp brown sugar

pickled garlic slices, to serve (optional)

1 Drain the tofu and pat dry with paper towels. Cut into ¾ inch/2 cm cubes.

COOK'S TIP

Buy firm, fresh tofu for this dish—the softer "silken" type is more like junket in texture and not firm enough to hold its shape well during cooking. It is better for adding to soups.

2 Heat the oil in a large skillet or wok and stir-fry the garlic for 1 minute. Remove the garlic from the skillet and add the tofu, then cook quickly until the tofu is well browned, turning gently to brown on all sides.

3 Lift out the tofu, drain well, and keep it hot. Stir the carrot and bell pepper into the same skillet or wok and stir-fry the mixture for 1 minute.

4 Spoon the carrot and bell pepper onto a dish and pile the tofu on top.

5 Mix together the chile, soy sauce, lime juice, fish sauce, and sugar, stirring until the sugar is dissolved.

6 Spoon the mixture over the tofu and serve topped with slices of pickled garlic. Serve hot.

Mango & Lemon Grass Syrup

This is a simple, fresh-tasting fruit dessert that rounds off a rich meal perfectly. Serve the mango lightly chilled.

NUTRITIONAL INFORMATION

Calories . . . . .117 Sugars 30g
Protein . . . . .1g Fat 0g
Carbohydrate . . .30g Saturates 0g

 15 mins   5 mins

SERVES 4

I N G R E D I E N T S

2 large, ripe mangoes

1 lime

1 lemon grass stem, chopped

3 tbsp superfine sugar

1 Halve the mangoes, remove the seeds, and peel off the skins..

2 Slice the flesh into long, thin slices and gently arrange them in a wide serving dish.

3 Remove a few shreds of the rind from the lime for decoration, then cut the lime in half and squeeze out the juice.

4 Place the lime juice in a small pan with the lemon grass and sugar. Heat gently without boiling until the sugar is completely dissolved. Remove from the heat and allow to cool completely.

5 Strain the cooled syrup into a pitcher and pour evenly over the mango slices.

6 Scatter the mangoes with the lime rind strips, cover, and chill before serving. Serve chilled.

COOK'S TIP

If you are serving this dessert on a hot day, particularly if it is to stand for a while, place the dish on a bed of crushed ice to keep the fruit and syrup chilled.

Exotic Fruit Salad

This colorful, exotic salad is infused with the delicate flavors of jasmine tea and ginger. Ideally, it should be chilled about an hour before serving.

NUTRITIONAL INFORMATION

Calories 65   Sugars 16g
Protein ....1g   Fat 0g
Carbohydrate ...16g   Saturates 0g

15–20 mins   0 mins

SERVES 6

INGREDIENTS

1 tsp jasmine tea

1 tsp fresh ginger root, grated

1 strip lime rind

½ cup boiling water

2 tbsp superfine sugar

1 papaya

1 mango

½ small pineapple

1 starfruit

2 passion fruit

1 Place the tea, ginger, and lime rind in a heatproof pitcher and pour over the boiling water. Let stand to infuse for 5 minutes, then strain the liquid.

2 Add the sugar to the liquid and stir well to dissolve. Let the syrup stand until it is completely cool.

3 Halve, deseed, and peel the papaya. Halve the mango, remove the seed, and peel. Peel and remove the core from the pineapple. Cut the fruits into regular, bite-size pieces.

4 Slice the starfruit crosswise. Place all the prepared fruits in a wide serving bowl and pour over the cooled syrup. Cover the bowl with plastic wrap and chill for about 1 hour.

5 Cut the passion fruit in half, scoop out the flesh, and mix with the lime juice. Spoon over the salad, and serve.

COOK'S TIP

Starfruit have little flavor when unripe and green, but when ripe and yellow they are sweet and fragrant. The tips of the ridges often turn brown, so run a vegetable peeler along each ridge before slicing.

Rose Ice

This delicately perfumed sweet granita ice, which is coarser than many ice creams, looks pretty piled on a glass dish with rose petals scattered over.

NUTRITIONAL INFORMATION

Calories 76   Sugars 9g
Protein ....2g   Fat 4g
Carbohydrate ....9g   Saturates 3g

15–20 mins, plus freezing   5 mins

SERVES 4

I N G R E D I E N T S

1¾ cups water

2 tbsp coconut cream

4 tbsp sweetened condensed milk

2 tsp rosewater

a few drops pink food coloring (optional)

pink rose petals, to decorate

1 Place the water in a small pan and add the coconut cream. Heat the mixture gently without boiling, stirring constantly.

2 Remove from the heat and allow to cool. Stir in the condensed milk, rosewater and food coloring (if using).

3 Pour into a freezeproof container and freeze for 1–1½ hours until slushy.

4 Remove from the freezer, and break up the ice crystals with a fork. Return to the freezer and freeze until firm.

5 Spoon the ice roughly into a pile on a serving dish and scatter with rose petals to serve.

COOK'S TIP
To prevent the ice from thawing too quickly at the table, nestle the base of the serving dish in another dish filled with crushed ice.

Lychee & Ginger Sherbet

A refreshing dessert after a rich meal, this sherbet is easy to make and can be served on its own or as a cooling side dish

NUTRITIONAL INFORMATION

Calories	159	Sugars	........40g
Protein	.........2g	Fat	...........0g
Carbohydrate	...40g	Saturates	.......0g

15–20 mins   0 mins

SERVES 4

INGREDIENTS

2 x 14 oz/400 g cans lychees in syrup

rind of 1 lime, finely grated

2 tbsp lime juice

3 tbsp candied ginger syrup

2 egg whites

TO DECORATE

starfruit slices

slivers of candied ginger

1 Drain the lychees, reserving the syrup. Place the fruits in a blender or food processor with the lime rind, lime juice, and candied ginger syrup and process until completely smooth. Transfer to a mixing bowl

2 Mix the purée thoroughly with the reserved syrup, then pour into a freezerproof container and freeze for 1–1½ hours until slushy in texture. (Alternatively, use an ice-cream maker.)

3 Remove the sherbet from the freezer and whisk to break up the ice crystals. Whisk the egg whites in a clean, dry bowl until stiff, then quickly and lightly fold them into the iced mixture.

4 Return to the freezer and freeze until firm. Serve the sherbet in scoops, with slices of starfruit and candied ginger to decorate.

COOK'S TIP

Do not serve raw egg whites to very young children, pregnant women, the elderly, or anyone weakened by chronic illness. If you omit them from this recipe, freeze the sherbet again and whisk it a second time to ensure a light texture.

Cardamom & Lime Pineapple

Thai pineapples are sweet and fragrant, and this local fruit appears regularly as a dessert, always skillfully sliced and carefully presented.

NUTRITIONAL INFORMATION

Calories 93	Sugars 23g
Protein 1g	Fat 0g
Carbohydrate . . .23g	Saturates 0g

 10–15 mins | 5 mins

SERVES 4

INGREDIENTS

1 pineapple

2 cardamom pods

1 strip lime rind, thinly pared

1 tbsp brown sugar

3 tbsp lime juice

mint sprigs and whipped cream, to decorate

1 Cut the top and base from the pineapple, then cut away the peel and remove the "eyes" from the flesh. Cut into quarters and remove the core. Slice the pineapple lengthwise.

2 Crush the cardamom pods in a pestle and mortar and place in a pan with the lime rind and 4 tablespoons of water. Heat until the mixture is boiling, then simmer for about 30 seconds.

3 Remove from the heat and add the sugar, then cover and let stand to infuse for 5 minutes.

4 Stir in the sugar to dissolve, add the lime juice, then strain the syrup over the pineapple. Chill for 30 minutes.

5 Arrange the pineapple on a serving dish, spoon over the syrup and serve, decorated with mint sprigs and whipped cream.

COOK'S TIP

To remove the 'eyes' from pineapple, cut off the peel, then use a small sharp knife to cut a V-shaped channel down the pineapple, cutting diagonally through the lines of brown 'eyes' in the flesh, to make spiralling cuts around the fruit.

Bananas in Coconut Milk

The Thais like to combine fruits and vegetables, so it is not unusual to find mung beans or baby corn mixed with bananas or other fruits.

NUTRITIONAL INFORMATION

Calories 157	Sugars 36g
Protein 2g	Fat 1g
Carbohydrate ...38g	Saturates 0g

10 mins   5 mins

SERVES 4

INGREDIENTS

4 large bananas

1½ cups coconut milk

2 tbsp superfine sugar

pinch of salt

½ tsp orange-flower water

1 tbsp fresh mint, shredded

2 tbsp mung beans, cooked

mint sprigs, to decorate

1 Peel the bananas and cut them into short chunks. Place in a large pan with the coconut milk, sugar, and salt.

2 Heat gently until boiling and simmer for 1 minute. Remove from the heat.

3 Sprinkle the orange-flower water over, stir in the mint, and spoon into a serving dish.

4 Place the mung beans in a heavy-based skillet and place over a high heat until turning crisp and golden, shaking the pan occasionally. Remove the mung beans from the skillet and crush them lightly in a pestle and mortar.

COOK'S TIP

If you prefer, the mung beans could be replaced with flaked, toasted almonds or hazelnuts.

5 Sprinkle the toasted mung beans over the bananas and serve the dish warm or cold, decorated with a few sprigs of fresh green mint.

Thai Rice Pudding

This Thai version of rice pudding is mildly spiced and creamy, with a rich custard topping. It's excellent served warm, and even better the next day.

NUTRITIONAL INFORMATION

Calories 351   Sugars 16g
Protein . . . . .7g   Fat 21g
Carbohydrate . . .37g   Saturates 16g

20 mins

1hr 30 mins

SERVES 4

INGREDIENTS

½ cup short-grain rice

2 tbsp palm sugar

1 cardamom pod, split

1¼ cups coconut milk

⅔ cup water

3 eggs

1 cup coconut cream

1½ tbsp superfine sugar

fresh fruit, to serve

sweetened coconut flakes, to decorate

1 Place the rice and palm sugar in a pan. Crush the seeds from the cardamom pod in a pestle and mortar and add to the pan. Stir in the coconut milk and water.

2 Bring to a boil, stirring to dissolve the sugar. Lower the heat and simmer, uncovered, stirring occasionally for about 20 minutes until the rice is tender and most of the liquid is absorbed.

3 Spoon the rice into 4 individual ovenproof dishes and spread evenly. Place the dishes in a wide roasting pan with enough water to come about halfway up their sides.

4 Beat together the eggs, coconut cream, and superfine sugar, and spoon the mixture over the rice. Cover with tinfoil and bake in a preheated oven to 350°F/180°C for 45–50 minutes until the custard sets.

5 Serve the rice puddings warm or cold, with fresh fruit and decorated with coconut flakes.

COOK'S TIP
Cardamom is quite a powerful spice, so if you find it too strong it can be left out altogether, or replaced with a little ground cinnamon.

This is a Parragon Publishing Book
This edition published in 2003

Parragon Publishing
Queen Street House
4 Queen Street
Bath BA1 1HE, UK

ISBN: 1-40540-880-4

Printed in China

NOTE

This book uses metric and imperial measurements. Follow the same units
of measurement throughout; do not mix metric and imperial.
All spoon measurements are level: teaspoons are assumed to be 5 ml, and
tablespoons are assumed to be 15 ml. Unless otherwise stated,
milk is assumed to be full fat, eggs and individual vegetables such as potatoes
are medium, and pepper is freshly ground black pepper.

The nutritional information provided for each recipe is per serving or per person.
Optional ingredients, variations or serving suggestions have
not been included in the calculations. The times given for each recipe are an approximate
guide only because the preparation times may differ according to the techniques used by
different people and the cooking times may vary as a result of the type of oven used.

Recipes using raw or very lightly cooked eggs should be
avoided by infants, the elderly, pregnant women, convalescents,
and anyone suffering from an illness.

The publisher would like to thank
Steamer Trading Cookshop, Lewes, East Sussex, for the kind loan of props.